The Art and Architecture of Herbert B. Turner

A Creative Odyssey

by Michael Gosney

WATERSIDE PRESS

WRITING TEAM: KEN COUPLAND, TAMAR LOVE, BINDU MOHANTY
BOOK DESIGN AND PRODUCTION: JOHN ODAM
EDITOR: LINNEA DAYTON
PHOTOGRAPHY: CRAIG MCCLAIN

FIRST EDITION

LIBRARY OF CONGRESS CONTROL NUMBER: 2007938456
ISBN 10: 1-933754-58-3
ISBN 13: 978-1-933754-58-1

WATERSIDE PUBLISHING
2376 OXFORD AVENUE
CARDIFF-BY-THE-SEA, CA 92007
WWW.WATERSIDE.COM

HEADLINE GRAPHICS
PRINTED IN KOREA

DEDICATED TO THOSE WHO
FOLLOW THEIR CREATIVE
CALLING – AND *DO THE WORK*.

ACKNOWLEDGMENTS

This book is the product of many people's work, including my fellow wordsmiths, whose contributions were invaluable. Sincere thanks to Tamar Love for her vital help in outlining the book and her extensive research and writing on Herb Turner's early years, Ken Coupland for his contributions to the architectural topics, Bindu Mohanty for her critiques and text additions and refinements, and Al Boeke for his sections on the Sea Ranch.

I am indebted to my colleagues, who all live, fittingly, in the Del Mar area, which harbors a lively community of publishing professionals. The team: master book designer John Odam, editor extraordinaire Linnea Dayton, photographer Craig McClain, publisher Bill Gladstone, printer Jerry Anderson, and our mutual friend, writer and publishing savant Gene Schwartz, who encouraged the idea for a book and originally introduced me to Herb. Special thanks also to the Turner family for their enthusiastic support and involvement at every phase of the book's development.

v

C O N T E N T S

vii

HERBERT B. TURNER

Citizen Artist and Builder

In this book Michael Gosney tells of the life and work of Herbert Turner, a gifted twentieth-century artist and builder, rooted in the classic traditions of his forms, inspired by the power of ideas, actualizing his vision through the world around him. By the skillful weaving together of the threads of Turner's insights and experience in his own words, and with supporting illustrative albums, Gosney offers the reader a series of invaluable lessons on how the principles governing the practice of art and architecture intersect, how these disciplines shape and express the quality of life in a community, and, above all, how the determined student can assemble the expert learning and apprenticeships that will frame a lifetime of creativity.

Turner is not a man who set out to change the world. Rather, as his story shows, it is through living for his own sake in the largeness of his soul and the genius of his craft that he has contributed throughout his lifetime to lifting the spirits and bettering the lives of others. In the process of his self-development, his mission has been to reveal to people what is possible, to show them their worthiness through art and their potential for a good life in harmony with their natural environment.

Writing of himself in 1974, Turner said, "I may be described as a traditionalist . . . what interests me are not ideas that swoop down upon us with swift suddenness, enrapture us momentarily with their novelty, and then just as quickly fade away, but ideas that will remain for a long period of time." He introduces us to the historic roots of his craft from the ideas of Eugene Emmanuel Viollet-le-Duc, Louis Sullivan and Frank Lloyd Wright to the sensibilities of Thomas Hart Benton, Edward Hopper and Andrew Wyeth.

Turner is shown not only to have been mentored by masters, but also to have worked hard to master the techniques of his art and his craft, from learning how to mix the pigments used in egg tempera painting, to perfecting the techniques of setting foundations in sandstone ravines.

Turner uses his art medium to comment on and express his sensibilities about the society around him as well as those close to him. Some of his most absorbing and affecting paintings are those he did while his son Brent and daughter Rachel were growing up.

Patiently observant and focused on the practical as well as the meaningful, Turner has been involved in civic affairs and cultural activities in his adopted home town of Del Mar, California. He is a man of his neighborhood and not of the ivory tower.

The circumstance of our meeting was probably inevitable. My publisher friend Dick Roe was a Del Mar activist leading a campaign to limit San Diego development, and for those reasons, he wanted me to meet a man who had become known as the area's most perceptive vote-getting bean counter. That was Herb Turner, who could produce a list that profiled the political leanings of every registered voter in the town.

We met at Carlos and Annie's, a coffee shop in the center of the city on a corner just across from what was at the time one of the most valuable vacant lots in Southern California—the site of the old Hotel Del Mar that had been demolished in 1969. In its hey-day before and just after World War II, it had attracted Hollywood greats of the era such as Bing Crosby, Pat O'Brien, Bette Davis, Jimmy Durante, Desi Arnaz and Lucille Ball— some of whom, in the 1930s, sponsored the construction of the Del Mar Race Track and fairgrounds at the mouth of the San Dieguito Lagoon.

Del Mar is a two-and-a-half-square-mile California seaside jewel, whose largest payroll expense when we met was devoted to its planning and lifeguard departments. It has the most beautiful stretch of accessible public beach anywhere along the coast from Mexico to Canada. Its breathtaking sunsets can' be viewed daily by strollers along its fifty-foot-high beachside bluffs as well as by passengers on the Los Angeles to San Diego Amtrak that snakes along its coastline on the old Santa Fe Railroad tracks.

This fiercely independent city was determined to preserve its residential qualities and the natural ecology of the seashore, lagoon and bluffs that anchored it. Its political conflicts, typical of many communities, centered not so much on community objectives but on the degree and kinds of regulations used to achieve them. That Herb would become absorbed by its political undercurrents was inevitable. It was a prize worth celebrating.

Well before we met, Herb Turner had a book inside of him that wanted to tell his story. He had already done an outline and a design treatment and sample pages several years earlier, having by then built some noteworthy houses and held several well-received gallery showings of his paintings. The book was awaiting a next step.

Our meeting was, in a way, a gateway to that next step, which then stretched over a thirty-year span. During that time I came to know, love and admire this man for his humanity and his gifts, and for the paradox of his simplicity of conversational expression and subtlety of thought.

Over the years, we discovered a kinship in the world of ideas and dreams. Our California experience at a time when self-realization movements were proliferating opened us to examining and challenging our world view and values from many angles. Suffice it to say that such California-born formulations as "win-win" and "living inside of the question" were not so much transformative for either of us, as they were revelatory in expressing intuitions and attitudes we had already recognized in each other. Werner Erhard and the EST movement challenged our more risk-averse conservative instincts.

We found a mutual affinity in our admiration for such individualist thinkers as the architect Louis Sullivan and the writer Ayn Rand, as well as for the exponents of liberal democracy among the founders of our nation. We were strongly wedded to the importance of a community in a free market that also guarded its natural heritage and maintained a civil society. While I was writing columns for the *Del Mar Surfcomber* quoting the Federalist Papers and Tocqueville, Herb was lining up votes for adoption of the referendums that made possible the elegant hotel and the ingenious multi-level shopping plaza, with their public spaces and view points, that now frame the downtown intersection of Del Mar where we first met.

By the time I returned from Del Mar to the Hudson Valley in 1992, we had spent many an hour strategizing, electioneering and organizing for consensus-building initiatives among the major factions in town. We engaged in highly spirited and contentious campaigns over local ordinances and referendums that shaped the character of the city as it exists today.

The book inside of Herb was the story of his experience and his creative development growing up in the Adirondacks in New York State, graduating from West Point and studying painting and sculpture at the Art Students League, then traveling west to Del Mar, to apprentice with John Lloyd Wright as an architect, and to build the life of an artist and builder around this captivating community.

A self-described traditionalist and regionalist, Turner is actually a radical presence in a world of art and architectural design seeking for universals attached to no idea, place or object anyone might recognize. While the mainstream of the contemporary art world celebrated Cubism, Expressionism, abstraction and the art of found objects, Turner was painting representational landscapes, figures and scenes using painstaking techniques in brushwork. Each of his paintings tells, through its composition and symbolism, a coherent story about its subject. While homes in the southwest were being built by formula to express a "southwest style," with developers bulldozing and leveling hills and valleys to accommodate the theme-park qualities of the new communities, Turner was designing homes and commercial buildings to rest comfortably within the contours of their natural settings, preserving the landscape, vegetation and ecology of the place.

Turner's most significant engagements with the community have happened because he couldn't resist getting something useful done about things that he cared for—usually creating a facility, getting a process going or finding the resources to accomplish a task. In 1975 when the City of Del Mar decided to revise its Community Plan, Turner was among those actively involved in its development. Ten years later he was once more deeply engaged in developing an update to the plan, *Del Mar 2000*, that was published as a vision of the future. In 1981, after Del Mar negotiated its cable television franchise, Turner contributed at no charge management and supervision of the construction of the cable TV studio funded by Daniels Cablevision. When the city was inviting design proposals for a new library–city hall complex, Turner was there with a *pro bono* low-cost alternative to various other proposals received by the city. When the venerable La Jolla Athenaeum Music and Arts Library wanted to expand and broaden its outreach into the community in 1996, Turner brought them together with the New School of Architecture and Design in San Diego to explore ways of collaborating in a new arts curriculum. In each of these community interactions, Herb's payoff was the utility of the outcome to himself and his community.

Turner's landmark contribution to the quality of life and village experience in Del Mar is Southfair, an elegant low-profile, all wood office cluster on the lowlands across from the race track and lagoon on the north side of town, with the added bonus of a sculpture garden and an outdoor art gallery designed into the inner courtyard of the complex. After an eight-year struggle to persuade the California Coastal Commission, as well as some of the city's resident preservationists, the three-and-a-half-acre development was built and became the community asset that it remains today. Sponsored by Turner, the gallery displays are periodically replaced and curated for local art, photography and architectural exhibits.

Herb Turner's artistic sensibilities are much in harmony with Auguste Rodin's advice given in his "Testament to a Young Artist," which Turner translated in his student days and which appears on pages 42 and 43. Rodin wrote:

"All is beautiful for the artist; for in all beings and all things his search penetrates to discover the character, that is to say the inner truth which hides under the form. And that truth is beauty itself. Study religiously. You cannot miss finding beauty, for you will meet truth."

Turner's life story as a citizen artist and builder has a satisfying and inspirational quality that seems to me almost perfectly expressed at the turn of the last century by the great Chicago architect Louis Sullivan. Sullivan paved the way for an American school of architecture that would break away from its European and classical influences and speak in the voice of the new nation. In his own life story, *The Autobiography of an Idea*, Sullivan wrote:

"The great creative art of up-building a chosen and stable civilization with its unique culture, implies orderly concentration and organization of man's powers towards this sole end, consciously applied in each and every one of his socially constructive activities in the clear light of his understanding that the actualities of good and evil are resident in man's choice — and not elsewhere. Thus will arise a new *Morale* in its might!"

The building blocks of a civilization are its countryside, villages, towns and cities. Those men and women who are in the service of Rodin's inner truth that lies under the form, and who move among their fellow citizens applying Sullivan's orderly concentration and organization of their powers toward the building up of their communities, those persons are the centurions who stand guard over our civic virtues and cultural heritage. Citizen Herbert Turner, artist and builder, is one of those guardians. His life and work can provide an instructive example for any student of the virtuous society.

Eugene G. Schwartz
Malden on Hudson, New York
October 2007

Eugene G. Schwartz is editor-at-large for *ForeWord Magazine*. Formerly a book publishing consultant and production executive, he was a resident of Del Mar from 1969 through 1971 and from 1978 through 1992. Between 1981 and 1995 he was a weekly columnist first for the *Del Mar Surfcomber* and then for the San Diego North County *Blade Citizen*.

This is the story of an American Everyman who followed his creative passions on an odyssey that led him from a Depression-era upbringing in upstate New York in a family of builders, to graduation from the West Point Military Academy, to an intense study of art in New York City, and then to an architectural apprenticeship with John Lloyd Wright in Del Mar, California. There, in the scenic coastal community that would become his life-long home and inspiration, Turner evolved as a pioneering architect-builder, master painter and successful businessman. Over several decades he has returned the inspiration to Del Mar, helping to set the stylistic tone of its distinctive organic-contemporary architecture, exhibiting his remarkable egg tempera paintings, and actively empowering the social and cultural fabric of his community.

I was intrigued with Herb Turner even before I met him. He was said to be a brilliant Renaissance man, a painter and sculptor, and an early Del Mar architect who had studied with Frank Lloyd Wright's son. As a resident of the San Diego region for many years, I had found Del Mar to be the place I was most drawn to. The architecture there, with its sensitive respect for the stunning natural environment, was one of the main attractions for me. I would soon learn that Turner had been a leading influence on this signature Southern California architectural aesthetic that combines natural woods, contemporary lines, large windows, dramatic indoor-outdoor spaces and, significantly, a deep ecological sensibility. Turner was, in fact, an early green architect, with his own "terramonic" philosophy that not only rejected the bulldozer in favor of undisturbed landscapes with houses integrated into the existing natural forms, but also encouraged with his designs interactions on many levels between the built and natural elements. This was a man I wanted to know.

With a background in publishing and digital media, I have had environmental leanings since the early 1980s when I published *The Life and Adventures of John Muir* by James Mitchell Clarke (Sierra Club Books, 1980) and Michael Tobias's *Deep Ecology* (Avant Books, 1984). As well, I've taken an active interest in large-scale green architecture for many years, serving on the board of urban designer Paolo Soleri's Arcosanti, a prototype green town and educational center in central Arizona, and co-founding the San Francisco–based Green Century Institute for sustainable communities. While my work with visionaries like Paolo Soleri has involved looking out ahead at the cities of the future, I found Herb Turner's practical but elegant approach to organic design to be resonant with the far-reaching ideas of eco-villages and "green cities." Soleri's "arcology" (architecture-ecology) ultimately rejects single-family houses in favor of multiple-housing solutions integrated within mixed-use complexes situated on open land. However, his approach to integrating the natural and built environments has much in common with Turner's basic "terramonic" philosophy (described on page 95 and implemented in the residential and commercial projects showcased in Chapter 2, "Designing Del Mar"). Arcology and terramonics share one fundamental principle, summed up by Turner's incisive observation that "people who love their homes sustain them." Both also demonstrate an overarching imperative: that the built environment and the organic landscape be integrated in a design that provides aesthetic and practical solutions that address the whole human as well as the whole of nature.

In getting to know Herb Turner, I quickly realized that he is more than a very talented architect and active community leader. He is also a true artist's artist. Early in his life Turner sought out and learned from his masters, and as he explored painting, sculpture and architectural design over 50 years, he would never compromise his creative process, and never lose his appreciation for and aspirations to the higher calling of art. Although he became a millionaire many times over during his career designing and building homes (and investing in real estate), he never considered the value of his creative work to be assessable in monetary terms. His thoughtful and carefully wrought egg tempera paintings, though widely exhibited, have mostly remained in his possession. His sculptural explorations have been ongoing and continue as he moves into his 80s (he was commuting weekly from Del Mar to Orange County for a sculpture class during the development of this book). As a designer-builder, he has always considered "build" to be the way to make money, while "design" is the creative side of the equation, and consequently he barely charged for the considerable time and energy he poured into the design phase of his every project with a determined tough love that would see his creative vision through the financing, permitting, planning and construction processes until the project was complete, almost always on time and under budget. In every case, after the dust settled, and after years and decades passed, the brilliance of his design solutions shone brighter the more life was lived within them.

Turner's approach to painting parallels in many ways his architectural process. Each painting can be seen as a design-and-build project, but in bringing a painting to life he is working for himself, calling upon his talent and his determination to better understand the human condition through an alchemical act of creation. As he does in designing a home, Turner plans and executes his paintings with a strong sense of depth and three-dimensional space. His sculptural apprehension of form and the delicacy of his egg tempera brushstrokes combine to realize the idea of the piece. His paintings (many are shown on pages 122 through 162) are thought-provoking works, exploring a wide range of the contemporary human experience, from subtle psychological relationships to social archetypes to political paradoxes. They embody an elegant complexity and depth. Though Turner has been identified as a Realist, and considers himself an American Regionalist painter in the tradition of Edward Hopper and Andrew Wyeth, his is a decidedly Californian approach to painting: His "region" is as much an interior world of expanding human reality and possibility as it is a formidable natural and cultural landscape.

Beyond architecture and painting, a third art form completes the Herbert Turner equation. Sculpture has been a deep discipline for Turner over the years. Although he early embraced painting as a more practical outlet—"a dozen eggs and some turpentine cost a lot less than bronze casting"—sculpture is perhaps the means of expression closest to his heart. A pivotal influence in his emergence as an artist was the work and philosophy of Auguste Rodin. This volume includes both Rodin's "Testament for a Young Artist," an impassioned call to artists that so inspired Turner that he was moved to translate the piece himself from the French (see page 42)—and Turner's commentary on it, "The Victory of the Truth Is Certain" (page 195).

Herbert Turner's creative odyssey has been a great inspiration to me, and I hope it will inspire many others through this book. His journey led him from the East Coast to the promise of a better life out West. Turner never looked back as he immersed himself in his new environment, and it did not take long for Turner to join the ranks of Californians who come to realize that "a better life" does not mean a better job or a better position in society, or even a better place to live. Making a better life, as Turner shows us, is about bettering oneself, and as a natural consequence bettering one's community and one's world. This is what has driven Turner in his life and in his art, to really *do the work*. The words of his Lehigh University wrestling coach Billy Sheridan still remind Turner to this day, as he labors quietly on a still-unfinished sculpture in his bright, airy studio: "Do the very best you can, and that is all a man can ask."

FINDING
A VOICE

If you want to be a singer, build a stage, crawl up onto it and start singing.
If you have a voice, people will come and listen. If not, then you will know.
—Frances Wright

Call it spunk, call it tenacity or sheer stubbornness, but Herbert B. Turner, in all that he does, in all his various incarnations of almost–army officer, artist and architect, lives by this dictum. Build the stage, get on it and express yourself. It's this determination that Turner showed growing up during the Depression years and graduating, against all odds, from West Point, one of the most rigorous military academies in the world. Since then, because a fateful accident prevented Turner from realizing his military ambitions, he has been using his hands, his eyes and his mind to express himself.

A talented painter, Turner employs unusual media, such as egg tempera—a painstaking technique that few contemporary artists use—to create symbolic stories, visual poems on board and canvas. As an architect, Turner, who trained under John Lloyd Wright, specializes in green architecture, creating simple but elegant structures designed in ways suggested by the landscape itself.

Turner looks back on his life's odyssey as a series of educational experiences that shaped his destiny—each important event a keystone in the structure of his life. Accordingly he recollects those incidents, those moments of clarity, when he learned something new about the world or about himself—a different perspective, an artistic influence or a moment of serendipity—that led him to explore new directions and uncharted paths.

Turner is totally absorbed in his work, which explains why he seldom vacations. "Why just go and look at something when you can be home doing something?" he wonders. "It's all about learning, improving yourself, setting your eyes on something and deciding you're going to do it—sports, politics, art, it's all the same."

The Early Years

Born in Mount Vernon, New York, in 1926, Herb Turner remembers the first time he actively learned a skill from someone other than his mother: At preschool in a neighbor's home he was taught to count. After preschool, Turner started school in Yonkers.

Although the stock market crashed when Turner was three years old, his family suffered no direct financial impact until 1932. When Turner was six years old, his parents, who owned a large house and several other properties in Yonkers, began to feel the financial burden of the Great Depression. Turner's bedroom on the second floor was rented out to strangers. Finally the family converted the basement into an apartment and moved there, alongside the furnace and the coal bin. His father built one more house. It did not sell. His father then moved to Saranac Lake to take care

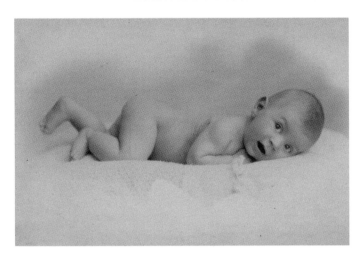

of family properties, while his wife Irene and their son stayed behind so she could manage the properties in Yonkers. What was meant to be only a brief separation continued, and nine-year-old Turner was sent to live with his father in Saranac Lake, in the beautiful and varied surroundings of the Adirondacks region of New York state.

HERB TURNER AS AN INFANT; MOUNT VERNON, NEW YORK, 1926.

SARANAC LAKE, NEW YORK, WHERE TURNER'S MOTHER'S FAMILY LIVED AND WHERE TURNER LATER LIVED AND ATTENDED SCHOOL.

The Depression was devastating to the parents of young children, but to the children themselves it was not as apparent. It wasn't until many years later when he read through the years of correspondence between his mother and father that Turner realized how hard they had struggled. He was deeply touched by this collection of letters, a very personal and telling recollection of the trauma of the Depression. His mother had tried hard to save all the properties under her management as she also carried the additional burdens of working as a maid, a housekeeper and finally a full-time assembly-line worker in a defense plant, like many women serving in the role of "Rosie the Riveter" during the war years. Turner never did live with his mother again, as his parents remained separated for more than fifteen years, finally reuniting after Turner had entered West Point.

Schooling at Saranac Lake

Turner remembers his Saranac Lake teachers as being very thorough and disciplined in their classes: "It was a time when student failure was not an option," he says. "No one wanted the stigma of being left behind."

After the sixth grade, Turner went to the junior high school in Saranac Lake, where he experienced different teachers and teaching styles. Attending a larger school also meant meeting a larger and more diverse pool of classmates—town kids, rural kids and children from the local Catholic grade school.

A warm, generous and energetic person, Turner had no problem making friends, often astounding people with his ability to be involved in so many activities at once and to do them all well. His teachers seemed to like him. Many had known Turner's mother when she was a student at the school. "But I was never given any special treatment," says Turner, "as much as I might have hoped for a little!"

During this period Turner also learned about the power of government. He remembers in particular one ninth-grade history teacher who inspired him with her talk on America's freedoms. Turner had never really given much thought to what it meant to live in America. Now, for the first time, he became aware of the freedoms of the individual, realizing that certain individual rights were greater than the power of the government. He saw American individual rights in stark contrast to the edicts of German and Russian rule, which were much in debate during the years leading up to World War II.

"For the first time," remembers Turner, "I understood that in the United States the government was a service to the individual, whereas in the other countries, the rights of the individual were secondary to the rights of the government. It was a huge concept—I remember being astounded that we, as adult citizens, would have so much power to change our country."

This knowledge empowered him with a tremendous feeling of self-worth, enabling him to believe he could change the unjust treatment of others if he gave it enough effort, and anchoring his commitment to civic duty and community, which he would carry throughout his life.

Unlike most other students, Turner experienced a steady influx of information from the outside world: He took his evening meals at a local boarding house that temporarily housed tuberculosis patients seeking the "cure" and single high-school teachers filling in for those leaving for military service. As new boarders arrived, there were discussions about politics, history, psychology, economics and various topics of the day. It was a very broadening experience for a high-school student.

A natural leader and organizer, in high school Turner devoted himself to numerous school organizations: He was on the baseball team and the football team and in the Boy's High Y and student government. He was a staff member of the school newspaper and business manager of the drama club, a responsibility that involved mounting theater festivals, working with a budget and keeping accounts. Furthermore, outside of school he was very active in the Boy Scouts organization as an Eagle Scout and summer camp counselor. It was challenging for Turner to participate in all these activities while keeping up with his studies, but he was inspired to do so by Miss Ruth Forth, the dynamic faculty advisor of the drama club, who rec-

TURNER'S HIGH-SCHOOL SENIOR PHOTOGRAPH, 1944.

ognized Turner as a multifaceted leader with the ability to manage a number of tasks simultaneously. Hearing Miss Forth's assessment of him further galvanized Turner to successfully accomplish a great many things concurrently.

Among the faculty members at the high school was a new teacher, Mr. Chuck Perry, the history teacher and sophomore student advisor. Mr. Perry was interested in giving his students the experience of the political process, which he said was significantly different than the teaching of political history. In order for the students to gain experience with the political process, Mr. Perry suggested to the sophomore class that they stage, with his guidance, a political takeover of all the school's organizations.

"We felt our class had the cohesiveness and leadership to really do it," Turner remembers fondly. "We wanted the political experience of running the school in a more dynamic way, and the best way of doing so was to make sure we were in control. Back then, we were all enthusiastic about making changes and doing things that really mattered. . . . I don't suppose that's changed a whole lot."

In his junior year, Turner and his classmates decided to follow Mr. Perry's advice and take over school activities, including the student government and the clubs. Consequently, this marked Turner's busiest year at high school: He participated in sports and served as class president, student council vice-president and business manager for the drama club. For his tenacity and dedication he won the school's loyalty prize at the year's end, which until then had never been awarded to anyone other than a senior. In addition, as a testament to Turner's versatility and involvement in diverse activities, the description of him in his high school yearbook reads, "A finger in every pie."

Also during his junior year Turner, for the first time, became aware of a real option for his future: pursuing his higher education at the United States Military Academy at West Point. Remembering what Miss Forth had told him about his leadership abilities and recalling her remark that the country's present leaders were all West Point graduates, Turner became determined to attend the academy.

At first, upon hearing of his decision, Turner's father was amused, noting that "No one in the Turner family has ever been to college." He felt that his son's grades were not good enough to gain admission. Instead of being discouraged, however, Turner was invigorated, accepting the challenge to prove to his father that he could accomplish his goal.

Bradens and Lehigh: Preparing for West Point

Support for Turner's ambition came through a friend. Harold "Brick" Bense, who had received an appointment to West Point, was an Eagle Scout

BRADENS PREPARATORY SCHOOL ENROLLEES, INCLUDING TURNER, THIRD FROM LEFT IN THE FRONT ROW.

in the same Boy Scout troop as Turner. Enlisting the help of his friend's father, a retired army lieutenant colonel, Turner began a rigorous academic program. Bense Sr. recommended that after high school Turner attend Bradens, a prep school designed specifically to prepare students for the exams leading to admission to West Point. With Bradens in mind and with a bit of luck and a lot of hard work, Turner was first in his congressional exam and fourth in the state exam, preliminary testing that earned him the opportunity to compete for West Point admission. Turner doubled up on his senior-year classes in order to complete his high-school education a full semester early, and raised his grade-point average to a respectable 92. Sadly, this meant giving up his extra-curricular activities, which he did reluctantly. However, his hard work was rewarded—after obtaining a three-month draft deferment so he could compete for a West Point appointment, Turner enrolled in Bradens.

Bradens was referred to as a "cram" school, partially because so much was crammed into a single day: Classes began at 8 a.m., broke for lunch at noon and then rejoined until 4:30 p.m. After a short dinner break, classes resumed again until 9:00 p.m. Saturday mornings were devoted to preparations for West Point admissions exams, after which the boys were granted the rest of the weekend off. In order to defray the high monthly costs of $350 for tuition, room and board, Turner daily waited on tables during breakfast, lunch and dinner, setting up for each meal, clearing away and washing the dishes afterwards. With this schedule, he had very little time for anything besides school and work. "At Bradens," Turner recalls, "there wasn't time for anything else. It was work, work, work, all the time. Nevertheless, we knew things would be even tougher at West Point, so it was good that we received a little taste of it at Bradens."

Despite his demanding schedule, it was at Bradens that Turner experienced an awakening of his artistic talents. Inspired by fellow student Dewitt Coulter, a hulking six-foot, 265-pound all-American football player who could wield a pencil with delicate grace, Turner began to draw with serious intent. Late at night he would go to his room and sketch for hours, basing his work on photographs, newspaper graphics and whatever else he could find lying around. Finally, in the wee hours of the morning, he would go to bed, only to get up a few hours later and wait tables. "I still don't know where I found the energy," Turner muses.

After winning first place in the appointment exam for West Point, Turner was elated that a year and a half of hard work had paid off. Unwilling to risk his West Point future on his ability to pass the entrance exam, Turner decided to enter West Point on a "dog ticket": He would go to another college for a semester to prove he could handle the experience of higher education; if his college grades were high enough, he could skip the West Point entrance exam altogether. Turner decided to attend Lehigh University, a college that had been suggested to him by both an academic professor at West Point and a local Ivy League artist, who also mentioned that the school had a great wrestling coach in Billy Sheridan.

Turner entered Lehigh in the fall of 1944 with the goal of achieving a high enough grade-point average to ensure his admission to West Point. Even though the coursework was difficult and the classes rigorous, Turner, ever the multi-faceted man, was able to participate in extra-curricular activities, joining the Delta Tau Delta fraternity as well as the football and wrestling teams. Wrestling coach Billy Sheridan's advice to "do the very best you can, and that is all a man can ask" proved to be an invaluable maxim throughout Turner's life.

Since Turner would not know for some time whether his Lehigh grades would be good enough, he took the additional precaution of returning to Bradens to study for the West Point entrance exam. When he received notice of his acceptance, he immediately began studying for his first year at West Point. Turner was admitted to West Point in the summer of 1945.

Starting Out at West Point

The first ninety days of a cadet's life at West Point, then known as "Beast Barracks," was as rigorous as or more rigorous than boot camp or basic training in the armed services. These first three months were meant to test a cadet's mettle and ensure he was really West Point material. If a cadet made it through the Beast Barracks and kept up with the academics,

BILLY SHERIDAN

While at Lehigh Universitys, Turner came under the influence of Billy Sheridan, the wrestling coach who created the proud tradition of wrestling at that university. Sheridan was a thin, red-faced, white-haired Scotsman of very few words, but when he spoke everyone listened.

When Turner was to wrestle in competition against the captain of the Coast Guard Academy team, Sheridan walked with Turner to the edge of the mat and then, staring off in the distance, said in a thick Scottish brogue, **"I know you haven't had a lot of experience, but I know you will do the very best you can, and that is all a man can ask."** Turner's anxiety vanished, he did his best, and he won the match.

Another time, when the team was returning to Lehigh from a Penn State match, conversation among the team members turned to wrestling colleges. When West Point came up, one wrestler, who knew Turner had received the appointment there, commented, "West Point is not a good wrestling school. They don't wrestle well— they're just strong. What do you think, Billy?" Quickly Sheridan replied, "If it's strength you have, then strength you should use."

And one day, one of the academic professors asked Billy how he got so much respect from his wrestlers, as he himself had failed to do so. Sheridan answered, "I treat them like men and they treat me like a man."

Fondly remembering Billy Sheridan, says Turner, "Of all the many thousands of words I heard at Lehigh, Billy's words are all that I can recollect exactly now, and they were well worth the trip."

TURNER ENTERING
WEST POINT: "BEAST
BARRACKS" BEGINS.

THE NEW PLEBE IN
BEAST BARRACKS
UNIFORM, ALMOST
THROUGH THE INITIAL
NINETY-DAY
TRAINING.

there was a good chance he could endure the discipline for the rest of the year. It was best to be seen as little as possible and heard even less. The only acceptable answer to any question was "Yes, sir!"; "No, sir!"; or "No excuse, sir!"

Cadet life at West Point was a highly structured and disciplined routine steeped in over 150 years of tradition. Advancement as a cadet was achieved and measured by making the fewest mistakes within a very narrow range of behavior: essentially eating, walking, dress, making grades and punctuality. The depth of one's voice and one's cadet friendships also reflected on one's military standing. Cadets were on the run all the time. Discipline was continuous.

When General Douglas MacArthur was superintendent at the Academy, he insisted that every cadet should be an athlete: "Upon the fields of friendly strife are sown the seeds that, upon other fields on other days, will bear the fruits of victory." Consequently, cadets had to be either on an intramural team, which competed with other cadets, or on corps squad teams, which competed with other colleges. Turner chose the corps squad because he reasoned, "If you have to play, why not play with the best you can?" Members of the corps squad sat at team tables, got a better diet and were relieved of many of the hassles of standard cadet life. "I planned to remove myself from cadet company discipline by qualifying for intercollegiate athletics," remembers Turner. "The plan was to play football in the fall, wrestle in the winter and play soccer in the spring."

Although Turner did pursue wrestling, his football career at West Point was short-lived. He made the C Squad, but quickly realized that trying to match his 155-pound frame to the other much larger football players was a very bad idea. He instead opted for soccer in both fall and spring. Unfortunately, Turner admits, he had no skill whatsoever at this sport. Determined to stay on the team, Turner did what he was best at: He tried harder. "The point is, I was willing to take a risk and try something for which I had no knowledge, talent or experience," Turner says. "I was willing to explore something new, and I once again bore in mind Billy Sheridan's advice that doing the very best you can is all you can ask of yourself. Following this principle, there was no fear of failure. You simply did the best you could at all times and judged yourself accordingly.

SATURDAY MORNING PARADE; CADETS RETURNING TO BARRACKS.

One of Turner's favorite pastimes at the academy was playing the familiar game of "beating the system," which primarily meant circumventing the copious regulations outlined in the Blue Book, West Point's cadet regulations manual. There were many ways to defy the Blue Book injunctions, such as putting clean laundry in the dirty laundry bag to avoid folding it, stealing pie out of the mess hall and going to reveille wearing pajamas and galoshes under the long winter coat. Turner knew that strict regulations were an essential part of military life, but felt that adaptability and creativity were equally essential.

On the Water

Soon Turner found a more meaningful way to express his urge for independent thinking and taking initiative. He decided to build a sailboat. The sole boat activity at West Point was the sailing club, and he found out that it was supported by a well-equipped shop on-base run by enlisted men. He dressed up in his best Saturday inspection uniform, went to the shop and asked who was in charge. When the top sergeant presented himself, Turner asked if there were any regulations against cadets using the shop. The sergeant thought for a few moments and said, "Not that I can think of," and then said, "we are here to train the cadets, but no cadet has ever asked."

Turner then asked, "Sergeant, may I have your permission to use these facilities to build something, under the conditions that I do not interfere with your work and that I work only at times you suggest?"

The sergeant became very curious and asked Turner what he was going to build. "A sailboat," Turner replied.

"How big is it?" the Sergeant asked.

"No bigger than those at the sailing club," Turner responded.

When he saw the sergeant frown, Turner quickly added, "But I only want to make the parts here. I will assemble them at a different location."

The Sergeant smiled and Turner had a deal. Now he only had to find a place where he could assemble the parts.

Growing up in Saranac Lake, Turner had always had boats that he fixed up each spring to use on the lakes in the summer, and this project put his experience to the test. As the boat began to take shape in the form of

TURNER AND STEVE WHITE AT WORK ON TURNER'S SAILBOAT.

18

numerous diverse parts, Turner chose to store them behind the basement lockers in the barracks. As the number of pieces in the store steadily grew, he moved the lockers out from the wall. The room kept getting smaller and smaller.

Finally, when all the parts were complete, Turner was ready to clear out the now-cramped locker room and start assembling the boat on a three-

day weekend when the rest of the cadet corps would be on parade in New York City. A sporting injury prevented Turner from accompanying the corps on the trip, so he spent that weekend assembling the boat under the stoop of the barracks. Hiding the unfinished boat was not an option, so he took the opposite course of action—"When you can't hide, be bold"—and displayed his work prominently. The response to the project was positive, and he encouraged inquiries. He was nearly ready to sail.

The Blue Book had no regulation prohibiting sailing your own boat down the Hudson River. Although Turner didn't know how to sail, he thought it seemed simple enough, so he gave it a try. While it was easy going down the Hudson with a good wind and a flowing current, getting

back up the river was another matter. When Turner realized he was already past the South Gate—there was *definitely* a regulation against passing that boundary—he began to panic. He turned the boat around and zigzagged to get back to the dock using a tacking maneuver, but the current going south to New York City was stronger than his tacking ability, which pushed him beyond panic. He tried to make for shore, with the idea of beaching the boat and scrambling back to the barracks. Fortunately, as he approached the shore, his tacking began to work. When he finally reached the sailing club docks, he ended his sailing career.

However, Turner was not finished with water altogether—not just yet. With two other cadets he would

plan a journey that retraced the post–Civil War expedition of Major John Wesley Powell on the Rio Grande. The three cadets would make the trip during their summer leave, traveling in folboats—light, collapsible crafts similar to kayaks.

20

RIDING THE RIO GRANDE

In 1947 Turner and two other cadets, Bruce Peters and Bob Pfeiffer, started planning a trip down 360 miles of the Rio Grande, in an area known as Big Bend Country in Texas. There was no record of anyone doing this trip since Major John Wesley Powell, the one-armed Union soldier who surveyed the Grand Canyon after the Civil War. In doing research in the Library of Congress to prepare for their trip, Peters found the journal of Major Powell's expedition with illustrations and graphic details that further motivated the effort. The cadets' trip, which was covered extensively in the July 1948 issue of *Pic* magazine ("The Magazine for Young Men"), began in Presidio, Texas, and ended at Adams Ranch on the border of Mexico. Negotiating the rapids in 2,000-foot-high Santa Helena Canyon (below) in their folboats—light, flat, collapsible watercrafts similar in appearance to kayaks—proved dangerous and difficult, yet exhilarating. The Rio Grande, known as "the world's driest river," was a difficult river to negotiate: Flash floods, as well as the mud, reeds and silt the river is infamous for, caused much trouble for the three cadets. Navigating was difficult, as was dealing with the harsh summer sun on the Texas-Mexican border, and a lack of drinking water and bathing opportunities in the muddy river. But just as he had met other challenges, Turner persevered and inspired his companions. The trip was a formative experience for them all.

FOLBOATS ON THE RIO GRANDE.

A Reawakened Desire for Art

When his initial year at West Point was over and he found himself no longer under strict discipline, Turner felt a sense of freedom. The "old, nagging desire" to be an artist arose again during his second year. Turner hoarded library books in his room, fashioning his own mini–art library of drawing texts. "From these books," Turner says, "I surmised that if you wanted to be a real artist, you had to study how to draw and paint."

Although West Point is a military establishment, Turner managed to find an art presence at the academy. The library contained monumental portraits of Washington, Adams and other heroes from the colonial period. While unable to identify personally with some of the library's great museum pieces, he loved Thomas Lea's paintings of the Panama Canal, which he found spontaneous and lively. He also admired the mess hall portrait gallery of former West Point superintendents, especially the portrait of General Douglas MacArthur. A number of artists he admired had connections to West Point: James McNeill Whistler, painter of *Arrangement in Grey and Black, No.1: Portrait of the Artist's Mother*, more commonly known as *Whistler's Mother*, was a West Point cadet who came from an army family; J. Alden Weir was an art instructor at West Point during the 1800s, as well as at Cooper Union and the Art Students League; and Peter Hurd, brother-in-law of Andrew Wyeth, who taught Wyeth the egg tempera painting technique, attended West Point and became a popular news correspondent during World War II.

After working his way through the drawing books, Turner was desperate to find an art instructor—someone who could really teach him something about painting. He longed for the kind of inspiring and critical instruction that he couldn't find in books. Working up his courage, Turner approached the head of the Military Topography and Graphics department, Colonel Lawrence Schick, for help. Schick referred him to Major Wilder, a commercial artist and teacher in the Graphics department. Wilder took him in and set him up with a pad, a hunk of charcoal and a plaster cast of a foot, and instructed the cadet to make a dozen drawings. After reviewing Turner's initial sketches, Wilder promoted him—now with a plaster head to draw before he was discharged. Turner had attracted the guidance he desired, even in this unlikely environment.

After meeting other cadets interested in painting, Turner did the only logical thing: He started a cadet art club, the first and only such group in the academy's 150-year history. Colonel Schick assisted him in finding a room with a skylight where Turner and his colleagues could meet and paint, and Turner beefed up membership by requesting and receiving weekend passes for club members to study art in New York City. When not enough cadets attended the club's art lectures, which consisted of art demonstrations and talks by invited guest artists, Turner held out a weekend pass like the proverbial carrot, requiring members to attend lectures if they wanted

THE WEST POINT ART CLUB, WHICH TURNER FOUNDED.

to go to the city. It worked. Numerous cadets began to attend, including Turner's roommate, Steve White.

On his first club trip to New York, Turner and the other club members had the opportunity to visit the studios of sculptor Adolph Weinman and portrait painter Sidney Lockman, both of whom were on the art advisory board at the Academy. The two gentlemen were not struggling artists in any sense of the term. Lockman had a very impressive two-story studio and sumptuous apartment on Central Park South. Weinman maintained two large English Tudor houses, side by side, one as his home and the other as his studio, the largest Turner had ever seen. "If this was the way artists lived," Turner quips, "then I was all for it." Next, he went for a three-hour drawing lesson at Mr. Naum Los's studio, where he received his first "formal" training.

TURNER ON MR. NAUM LOS

Some time before my art weekend, my mother contacted a school advisory service and was directed to the small painting and sculpture studio of Mr. Naum Los, at 22 E. 60th Street in New York. She had met with Mr. Los and arranged for me to see him when my West Point art club came to New York.

When I entered his studio, Mr. Los was wearing a painter's smock over his tweed street clothes. He wore a plastic visor, which he took off as he made a Continental bow, shaking my hand. He was a very soft-spoken, courteous Continental gentleman.

NAUM LOS

After a brief conversation, he ushered me into his studio, which was about fifteen feet by twenty feet, with a north-light studio skylight. There was a model stand on the south wall, surrounded by a row of low artists' easels and another row of taller easels. The model was an old man with a beard and a broad-brimmed hat that turned up in front.

This was the first time I had drawn a live model. I remembered my block-head drawings at West Point, but this model had no planes at all. The top of his head was covered with his hat, and his beard covered everything else, except his eyes and his nose.

Mr. Los must have recognized my anxiety, as he asked me if I had ever drawn from a live model before. My answer was a quick "No, sir." He gave me preliminary instructions on how to start, and then periodically came by and asked questions, like what did I think about the length of the nose—was it too long or too short?

Mr. Los did not appear to instruct. All he did was ask me questions and require me to look at the model for answers. When the session was over, I was amazed and puzzled at how well I had done. I didn't realize it at the time, but this was his way of requiring me to teach myself. The simplicity of his method completely eluded me then, but the results were apparent after this first three-hour session.

This was the beginning of my relationship with Mr. Los that would last three years after graduating, until he closed his school. He was an invaluable influence on my skills and approach, and inspired my self-confidence as an aspiring painter and sculptor.

FIRST DRAWING AT NAUM LOS STUDIO.

For the next two years, whenever he could get to New York by 9:30 a.m. on a Saturday, Turner took classes from Los. Unfortunately, since cadets had only a few weekends off each year, these lessons were rare.

After taking a few classes with Los and enlisting the interest and support for the art club from another West Point graduate, Colonel "Red" Reeder of the Tactical department, who was an avid painter, Turner began to think more seriously about his future. Was he a soldier-in-training or an artist emerging? He took his question to the military psychologist. Steeling himself as though he were about to confess a deadly sin to a chaplain, Turner instead found his artistic interest met with a warm reception.

"First, I wanted to know if my desire to become an artist was a reaction to the climate of discipline at West Point," Turner remembers. "I wanted to make sure this artistic drive wasn't just a temporary malady that would suddenly vanish after graduation." After speaking with the psychologist, Turner found his answer: His desire to be an artist was no different than any other creative person's wish to express himself in the medium to which he was most drawn.

The psychologist administered an aptitude test, which yielded surprising results. Turner was best suited for a career as an Army officer, an artist and an architect. "I was startled," Turner says. "The results seemed ridiculous. I could understand the combination of artist and architect, but the army officer component just didn't fit with the other two career options. I remember thinking something must have been wrong with the test."

The psychologist, however, was more interested in learning about Turner's latent architectural ability, which the cadet had never mentioned. "I told him my father was a builder and my mother drew up plans for houses until the Depression," says Turner. "My mother's father, Augustine Branch, was one of the most prominent builders in the Adirondacks in the late 1800s, and my father worked for his firm, Branch & Callaghan in Saranac Lake." The mystery was solved and the doctor's confidence in the test reaffirmed. Turner had no choice but to believe in the random-seeming combination of abilities the test defined.

"It was confusing at the time," Turner remembers, "But then after speaking further to the psychologist, it all became very clear. After all, I was attending West Point, the leading military school in the world. I shouldn't have been surprised the test recommended I train as an army officer. I was just having trouble understanding how I could do so and pursue the life of an artist."

His mentor, Colonel Schick, helped him work through this duality of purpose. The colonel had experienced the same quandary when he was a cadet, taking two months' leave after graduation from the academy to study

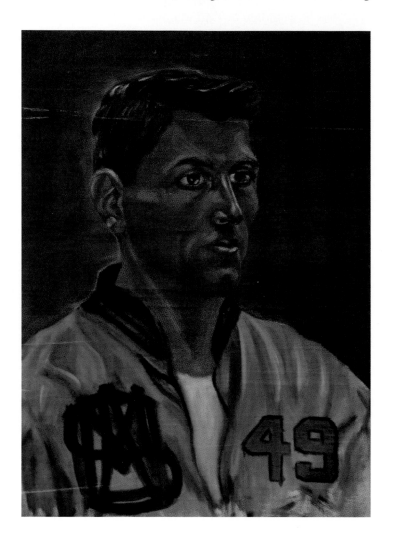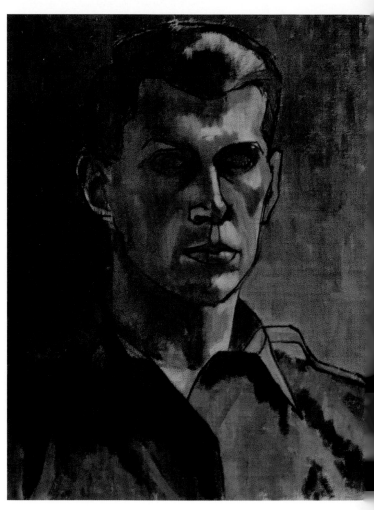

with a well-known etcher. After concluding there was no way he could earn a living as an artist, Schick had returned to his career in the army, continuing to enjoy his drawing and etching, which remained secondary passions.

While Turner respected the colonel's advice to wait until graduation before further pursuing his passion for art, he did not want to follow it. In the spring of 1948 Turner wrote to Robert Brackman, an artist he admired, and was accepted to join a two-week workshop during his summer leave in August. "When I was accepted," Turner says, "I was thrilled. I would have two solid weeks of painting, morning and afternoon, with the leading art teacher of the day, and a renowned artist himself." An astute and dedicated student (as he has been his entire life), Turner was excited to learn from someone who *did the work* as well as taught about it. He valued this quality greatly, and would seek it in all his mentors to come.

A Fateful Decision

In the spring of 1948 Art Doyle sought to enlist Turner's help in coaching his company's C-2 soccer team. Doyle would have to be the official coach but Turner would be given complete charge under all circumstances. Doyle wanted to win the Regimental Championships. At that time, all cadets were assigned to companies according to height. Company C-2 was the third shortest company and had difficulty in intramural athletics. Turner considered Doyle's offer for a while and then declined.

About a week later, Doyle appeared again in uniform, posing the question, "As C-2 company commander, I am asking if cadet Corporal Turner has given any more thought to the idea of returning to company C-2 to assist with soccer training."

Turner replied, "Sir, since you put it that way, could I further clarify my role?"

Turner then laid out his plan reminding Doyle that C-2 was rather short in stature, and that in the past the good athletes in the intramural program had been distributed throughout the various sports. Turner suggested that he alone would pick the best athletes and have them volunteer for soccer.

Doyle asked, "How would you get them to volunteer?"

Turner replied, "I would tell them Company Commander Doyle and Corporal Turner would appreciate their service, and that Corporal Turner is in charge of making the list of volunteers, along with the names of those who refused, which he will then hand to Commander Doyle.

Commander Doyle replied, "Good idea, Mr. Turner."

Turner had no inkling at the time that this decision would change the course of his entire life. He began his quest to recruit players for soccer without difficulty and had a few practices before competition. They won the first two games. The third game was with L-2, the second tallest of the

SELF-PORTRAIT OF TURNER PAINTED AT WEST POINT BEFORE HE STUDIED WITH ROBERT BRACKMAN.

SELF-PORTRAIT AFTER TWO WEEKS UNDER BRACKMAN'S INSTRUCTION.

companies in average height. The score was tied when, in an aggressive maneuver, a C-2 player inadvertently kicked an opposing L-2 player and broke his leg, sending him to the hospital. The C-2 player was benched. When the game resumed, C-2, although smaller, played with renewed vigor.

Turner was playing the right wing position when the ball was suddenly kicked in his direction and there was only one L-2 player in front of him. Both players ran as fast as they could and kicked as hard as they could.

Turner heard a loud cracking noise and looking down saw that his right shin guard—and his leg beneath it—were broken off to the right. He fell

to the ground and raised his right leg as high as he could and slammed it into the ground. The next words Turner heard were those of his roommate, Steve White, saying "It's all right, the leg is straight," as he held Turner's head to prevent him from thrashing about.

Turner was rushed to the hospital and given morphine, and soon had his leg in a cast. During his extended stay in the hospital, his leg was reset three times during the first month alone. By this time his doctor realized that a civilian specialist was required and Turner would have to authorize the procedure.

Turner asked, "What will happen if I don't sign?"

The reply was, "You will lose the lower part of your leg."

"If I do sign?"

"You will keep the lower part of your leg and you will be able to walk."

With a straight face Turner asked, "What do you recommend?"

The doctor's reply, "The operation," was also given with a straight face.

Turner replied with a smile, "Good decision, sir."

HIS LEG BROKEN IN A SOCCER GAME, TURNER BEGINS A YEAR-LONG RECOVERY, DURING WHICH, AGAINST DOCTOR'S ORDERS, HE WOULD ATTEND ROBERT BRACKMAN'S ART SCHOOL AND FIRMLY ESTABLISH HIS CAPABILITIES AS A PAINTER.

BRACKMAN'S SUMMER SCHOOL PAINTING CLASS IN NOANK, CONNECTICUT.

About mid-July, Turner asked his doctors if he could take leave to attend Brackman's summer school. The answer was a definite "no." The doctors were worried about the movement of the delicate bone graft in a bus, a car or even a train. Turner mentioned this problem to Steve White during one of his frequent visits.

White and Turner conceived a plan to have a hospital ambulance take Turner to the army airport at Stewart Field and then fly him just 250 miles to the Saranac Lake airport, 10 miles from his parents' home. Turner

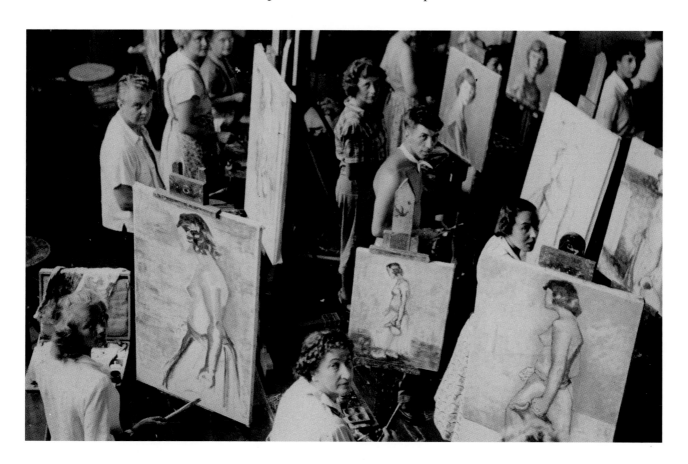

argued that he would rather spend a month with his parents than be stuck in the hospital all summer. The doctors agreed to this plan, and White went to Stewart Field and found a pilot who required more flying time.

After he was home for a couple of weeks, however, Turner convinced his parents to drive him about 300 miles to Brackman's school in Noank, Connecticut, and to pick him up two weeks later. It was a fruitful summer school experience for Turner, putting his artistic talents to the test. He finished the course at Brackman's with renewed enthusiasm for his potential as a painter and a general feeling of accomplishment on a new level.

ROBERT BRACKMAN

Robert Brackman was the teacher who helped Turner to galvanize his painting talents. In Brackman's summer painting school, Turner and thirty other students studied figure painting in the morning and still life in the afternoon. Brackman would pose the model in the morning and arrange the still-life pieces in the afternoon. At the beginning of the pose, everyone drew numbers for a position around the model. Then the monitors (his teaching assistants) would set up the studios, taking first choice of position. After that, other students would take their places according to the numbers they drew.

An enthusiastic and inspiring teacher, Brackman would give critical feedback every day, along with a demonstration in painting. Because of Turner's leg injury, he could not move around to look at the other paintings as Brackman critiqued them; instead he listened to the criticism and tried to incorporate this feedback into his own paintings before the instructor got to him.

Brackman's first instruction was oblique: He told one student not to paint the color he saw, but to paint air, the space between the student and the model, and the space between the model and the wall. Turner had absolutely no idea what Brackman was talking about—he was having enough trouble getting the modeling of the figure and some semblance of color. However, Turner had the good fortune to have been placed next to one of the advanced students. When he asked in a whisper how he was supposed to paint air, the student smiled and whispered back, "Add a little white." Brackman, who was instructing another student at that moment, said, "Don't add white, you will lose your color." Turner turned to his student advisor. He shrugged his shoulders and smiled.

Later, Turner came back to study with Brackman in New York for three years, until the master painter noted Turner had begun to paint in his own style, and urged him to paint on his own, to further nurture and develop his painter's "voice." Brackman was instrumental in establishing Turner's confidence and standing as a painter.

ROBERT BRACKMAN

TURNER'S FIRST OIL PAINTING UNDER BRACKMAN'S INSTRUCTION.

After his summer leave, Turner returned to West Point on crutches. In his last year, he began to realize his leg was not healing as well as it should have. The nerves in his leg had been so badly bruised by the accident that the entire surface of his foot was hypersensitive—just touching the skin made him jump. To combat this hypersensitivity, the doctors gave Turner spinal blocks, but these numbed the entire leg. The cure was proving to be worse than the ailment: Turner realized the procedures could be dangerous and of no long-term help in reducing the hypersensitivity.

Understanding that he needed to let his leg heal, Turner considered the possibility of taking the rest of the year off. In his condition, he would never pass the physical exam required for an army commission, and he still had not reconciled himself to the idea of being both an artist and an army officer. Consequently, he felt that if he could get medical dispensation after mid-year exams, he would have a full year to study art and allow his leg to heal. The time would allow Turner to sort out his feelings, test his aptitude in art and find his path, choosing between a career in the army and a career as an artist.

However, the commandant of cadets, Brigadier General Paul Harkins, felt differently. After listening to Turner plead his case, General Harkins reminded Turner that he was a West Point cadet training to be an army officer and stated that his taking time off to study art would not be in the best interest of the academy. He turned down Turner's request, telling him that his leg would heal and that he would graduate, pass the army physical and be commissioned.

Later in the year, when his leg had improved enough so that he was back in the barracks on regular duty, Turner was required to take another physical exam. Afterwards he proceeded to purchase his army uniform and plan for service in the army. But about a week before graduation, he received a phone call from General Harkins asking if he was the Turner who had failed the medical exam.

Turner replied, "No, sir. I took the exam many months ago and have not received a failure notice. I have purchased my uniform and am prepared for service."

General Harkins stated, "This report has been on my desk for ten days, and you haven't received it?"

Without thinking, Turner replied, "No, sir—probably because it has been sitting on your desk for ten days."

There was dead silence, during which Turner wished he could have reached into the phone and retracted his response.

General Harkins then commanded, "Mr. Turner, I want you to report to my office, right now."

Turner replied, "Sir, I have a class."

"Mr. Turner, do you know who you are talking to? I am General Harkins, the commander of the cadets."

"Yes, sir."

Turner arrived at the stairs to General Harkins's office just as the General and a group of officers were descending. He immediately slapped up against the wall, saluted and said, "Cadet Turner, reporting to General Harkins as ordered, sir." Without missing a step the General told Turner to meet with his adjutant upstairs for instructions. All the officers passed by and Turner leaned against the wall for a few seconds wondering if this was the formal ending of his six-year effort toward a military career.

When he entered the adjutant's office, he was instructed to sit down, and then the adjutant said, "I understand that you were notified of the surgeon general's report only now. That was unfortunate. I am sure you realize that this report is final and there is no appeal. If you do improve, I recommend that you do not attempt to come back into the service, for this injury will show up, and mid-way through your career you will be passed over by your juniors. It is much better to become a civilian now rather than later." The adjutant issued immediate leave for Turner to see his parents, arranged for transportation and wished him good luck. The meeting, marking a definitive end to Turner's military prospects, lasted no more than twenty minutes.

Before graduation Turner returned home to his parents' house in a state of shock to sort things out. "I could never have found an honorable way to leave the academy," Turner reminisces. "The moral commitment I had made to myself and to those who expected me to continue at the academy was stronger than my willingness to leave a safe and successful career to embark on one that was questionable, even tainted. My injury took the decision out of my hands."

WEST POINT CLASS OF 1949 GRADUATION.

Learning to Create

After working toward a military career for six years—first two years to get into West Point and then four years to make it through—the thought of finding a civilian profession was frightening. What Turner really wanted to do was study art, but after living through the Depression and World War II, when faced with the decision, he was not sure he wanted to risk his future on art.

Then he thought back to Adolph Weinman's and Sidney Lockman's opulent New York studios and reasoned that perhaps it *was* possible to make a decent living from the study of art. Still, he questioned his abilities. There was only one thing to do. Turner moved to New York City and began to study with his two mentors: Robert Brackman and Naum Los. As Turner continued his painting and sculpture studies, he was receiving his education from professionals who actually *did* the work as well as taught, just as he had experienced at West Point. His two mentors had stature in their professions equal to that of the West Point instructors.

Brackman taught classes at the Art Students League. He also started a class at the American Art School behind Carnegie Hall, one block from the League. Turner had been at the League only for a couple of months when Brackman chose him to be the monitor after observing his intense determination, and remembering him as a cadet in uniform and on crutches at his summer school. The monitoring position was prestigious, but more important, it meant that Turner would no longer have to pay tuition to study with Brackman. Although the war and the Depression were both over, Turner was living on a limited budget, and having a tuition waiver would greatly help. Besides, his father would be impressed by his getting a monitoring position after just two months.

Unfortunately, the school suffered a financial crisis and they were forced to vacate the building. Not one to let any obstacle stand in the way, Turner did a little networking and found a new studio from which Brackman could teach. Located at 427 E. 85th Street, the building was owned by the Countess Maria Zichy, who also taught classes there. After visiting the building, Brackman agreed it was a good studio but said that he would need ten easels.

"I will make them," Turner said and he did.

34

TURNER (LEFT) AND BRACKMAN (RIGHT) WORKING ON A FANCIFUL RUBENS MONTAGE INCORPORATING FACES OF THE NEIGHBORHOOD BUSINESS LEADERS.

Countess Zichy had come to the United States when Russian Communists took over Hungary. She related extraordinary stories about her life in Hungary. The stories were delightful to listen to, but Turner wondered if they were true.

Then one day Turner mentioned to the countess that he coveted a French painting box with a built-in easel that was for sale at Fredrick's art supply store on 57th Street, but which was still too expensive for him. The countess instructed him to ask Mr. Fredrick for a student discount. "After you get the discount," the countess continued, "say Maria Zichy sent you and see what happens." Turner did as he was told. Upon hearing Maria Zichy's name, Fredrick, with great enthusiasm, inquired, "Ah, how *is* the countess?" Then he launched into a half-hour story about the countess and her

husband the count. Turner's doubts about Maria Zichy were put to rest. He also received a further substantial discount on top of his student discount on the painting box and easel.

Turner later lived in one of the countess's apartments at 427 E. 85th Street that had been previously rented to the crown prince of Belgium, who was employed by the Metropolitan Museum of Art. Turner appreciated his situation: For a struggling art student he was doing quite well.

During this time, Turner was spending hours at Brackman's studio class, learning the painter's approach to painting. Brackman was a serious artist who had studied with Robert Henri and George Bellows, both famous teachers and painters who had influenced several generations of artists. Brackman was an admirer of the French painter Henri Fantin-Latour, an early Impressionist and a student of Horace Lecoq de Boisbaudran. Turner's other mentor, Naum Los, was also an enthusiastic admirer of Lecoq de Boisbaudran and had developed his teaching material directly from Lecoq's work.

However, Brackman and Los had two completely different teaching styles, and Turner felt this difference especially strongly when he was with Los. It was like studying with two parents, one in the morning and one in the afternoon, each of whom had a totally different heritage, philosophy and set of opinions. Turner felt like a child who respected both parents but was aware of the tension between the two.

Both Brackman and Los were Russian by birth, but their approaches to art were 100 years apart. Brackman was Jewish and had come to the States as a young immigrant, receiving his art education first in San Francisco and then in New York City. Los, a member of the professional class, was invited to the United States because of his reputation as a sculptor and

teacher in Rome. Los's very disciplined education was in Berlin, Brussels and Paris, with two years of dissection in Switzerland. Los spoke German, French, Italian, Russian and English fluently and was always the Continental gentleman.

While Brackman, who used contemporary techniques, didn't mind if Turner brought in ideas from Los's class, Los felt differently. He knew Turner was studying with Brackman, but he demanded the student adhere to his colorist approach, a technique of teaching that was 100 years old, instructing Turner to paint only the exact color he saw. In his own work,

Turner incorporated techniques from both men, further studying art and art history from books to examine the techniques of both instructors.

Although Turner had two instructors for painting, he was deficient in one essential area: drawing—a necessary building block of any artistic education. Challenged by Brackman to take two years of drawing, Turner went to the National Academy of Design for night classes under Ivan Olinsky, one of Brackman's early instructors.

During this intense educational period, Turner's days were full. He had painting with Los in the morning, painting with Brackman in the afternoon and drawing at the academy at night. He was in the studio working about nine hours a day. He tried to study five days straight, but by Wednesday he would be dead tired, so he would take the Thursday or Friday evening class off to be able to study sculpture on Saturday mornings with Los. Sunday was a day of total rest, and then on Monday it was back to work. On his few days off, Turner went to museums, especially his favorite, the Frick Collection, to recharge imagination and inspiration.

Turner had little spending money, but he got by. Brackman's classes were free because Turner was a monitor. Because of his West Point injury, he received New York state veterans funds, which paid for the classes he took with Los; and he had received a scholarship to attend drawing classes at the National Academy of Design. A government pension of $49 per month, a few dollars from his family and the $1 a night he made working at the academy art store paid his rent and living expenses. He lived simply, eating yogurt for lunch, which kept him invigorated during the day, and often pressure-cooking inexpensive ham-and-cabbage suppers, which he gulped down before evening classes.

His social life, too, was extremely limited during this period, but it did satisfy some of his need for personal interaction. He socialized only with art students. Though immersed in a rich artistic environment, Turner didn't go to New York galleries, but rather spent all his time learning technique. All he cared about was mastering the crafts of drawing, painting and sculpture. Neither Turner nor his friends considered themselves artists: They were art students, and perhaps one day in the future, after they had finished art classes, they could be artists. Turner felt strongly that it was essential to *learn* the language of art before he could really *speak* it.

As for those untrained people who were calling themselves artists and showing experimental work in popular galleries, Turner felt nothing but perplexity. "I just didn't understand artists who wanted to express themselves without having any artistic education," Turner says. "The artists in Greenwich Village seemed to be just a bunch of people who got together and drank coffee and talked art. My West Point education taught me to stay focused and to learn my trade. These other artists seemed a little goofy to me. Theirs was not the path I wanted to take."

Turner knew he was done with Brackman's classes when he began to paint differently from what he'd been doing for the past three years. Brackman painted color onto a white canvas; Turner began to paint on toned canvas, adding light to it. Turner's particular aesthetic told him that his way made a lot more sense. Brackman said it was okay to move on—Turner had finished his instruction and was ready to begin his private study. Brackman felt Turner would need ten years of painting by himself to become the artist he knew he was meant to be.

After three years of study, Turner had no idea what he would do with his art training. Like many people who pursue a passionate yet uncertain future in the arts, he figured he could teach someday, making enough money to support his artistic life. He felt he had taught himself to be a good teacher by talking to himself while he was painting, applying the same critical eye to his own painting as his instructors did, and learning how to analyze and improve his work. From Brackman and Los, Turner learned that an instructor does not teach his students in the manner that he himself paints, but rather in the manner that he was taught. Turner felt he would be able to emulate that teaching tradition and be a reasonably effective painting teacher.

Studying Rodin

Los was teaching Turner painting, but only a little bit of sculpture, a subject in which Turner felt the need for a more thorough grounding. Turner admired the American sculptors Augustus Saint-Gaudens, Daniel Chester French and Anna Hyatt Huntington, but it was Auguste Rodin he admired most. "If Rodin hadn't sculpted," Turner says, "I never would have sculpted."

TURNER'S FINAL DRAWING AT THE NATIONAL ACADEMY OF DESIGN, 1951.

Noting Turner's interest in Rodin, Los instructed him to study Rodin's early work. Los felt that it's in a master's early work that a student can discover how he became a master. Then if one is really determined, Los taught Turner, one should study the work of the master's teacher, if one can find out who he was and what he thought. Turner felt doubly blessed that Los had studied both Rodin and Rodin's teacher, Lecoq de Boisbaudran.

When Turner asked Los for material on Rodin, Los recommended that he read Paul Gsell's conversations with Rodin, translated into English. Turner read this book with great enthusiasm. When Los borrowed the English translation Turner had read so he could compare it to the original French, both men were surprised to find that the French edition had an additional chapter. Im-mediately interested in discovering what this ex-tra chapter would reveal, Turner asked Los if he would translate it for him. Los declined, be-cause he felt this impor-tant writing would have more meaning for Turner if the student

ONE OF TURNER'S LAST SCULPTURES WITH LOS, WHO HAD TAUGHT HIM TO THINK IN THREE-DIMENSIONAL SPACE, FOLLOWING RODIN'S APPROACH AS INSPIRATION.

40

translated it himself. The result, translated by Turner as "Testament for the Young Artist," has been an inspiration and a touchstone for Turner throughout his professional life. (The "Testament" is included here on pages 42 through 43, and Turner's additional thoughts about Rodin are included in an "Appendix" at the end of this book.)

Turner studied sculpture with Los for only a few months after leaving Brackman's studio. Then, much to Turner's surprise, Los retired and de-cided to move to Florida. Some of his students planned to move to Florida as well if Los decided to teach a few classes a week in a studio that the students planned to set up in Los's garage. Turner, however, decided against moving to Florida until Los was settled. Instead he spent that summer at home in Saranac Lake with his parents.

LECOQ DE BOISBAUDRAN AND AUGUSTE RODIN

Horace Lecoq de Boisbaudran (1802–1897) used what many think is the most effective method for teaching art. A believer that art was created by using human feeling and genius to observe and interpret the artist's subject, Lecoq held forth two maxims with regard to the relationship between teacher and student: "Art is essentially individual . . . individuality makes the artist," and "All teaching . . . must make it its aim to keep the artist's individual feeling pure and unspoiled, to cultivate it and bring it to perfection." By nurturing each student's individual creativity, genius, feelings and perceptions, Lecoq trained students who were able to see an object, reproduce it exactly and then use their own abilities to make art out of it.

Memory was key to Lecoq's method of teaching. Developed to teach adolescent students to draw in preparation for their careers as tradesmen, Lecoq's method involved having students draw a one-inch line with a ruler. After drawing the line with the ruler many times, the students were told to put away the ruler and draw the same line freehand. When they were adept at re-creating the one-inch line, Lecoq had them combine more lines and create one-inch-square boxes. From there, the students learned to draw other shapes, always with the same basis and always in freehand only after exhaustive study with some similarly shaped object. Soon the students could draw almost anything after seeing it once..

Lecoq's art students were told to memorize a painting, and then to draw it from memory, which they could do after training with Lecoq, who was often called Papa Lecoq. "In observing a subject," Lecoq writes, "there are five principal points to be kept in view . . . dimensions, position, form, modeling and color." By teaching these principals, Lecoq was able to train students who were so adept at memory drawing that when challenged by college-aged art students at the Ecole des Beaux-Arts, the most prestigious art school in France, Lecoq's much younger students won with ease.

One of Lecoq de Boisbaudran's most famous pupils, Auguste Rodin, never went to Ecole des Beaux-Arts. He applied and was rejected three times for his sculpture. Rodin studied with Lecoq, who remembered his former pupil fondly. Rodin, possibly the best-known sculptor in the world, went on to create *The Thinker, The Kiss* and hundreds of other works of art, and served as the primary source of inspiration for Turner's sculpting efforts.

LECOQ'S TEACHING METHOD EMPHASIZED MEMORY, AS EXEMPLIFIED BY THIS STUDENT'S WORK, DRAWN ENTIRELY FROM MEMORY.

"TESTAMENT FOR A YOUNG ARTIST" BY AUGUSTE RODIN, TRANSLATED BY HERBERT B. TURNER

In deep appreciation to my teacher, Mr. Los, deeper than words can ever express, for having introduced me to this precious message, I present to all artists, everywhere, for their enlightenment and pleasure, the "Testament" of Auguste Rodin.

—Herbert B. Turner

Young people who wish to be the officials of beauty, perhaps you will find here a resumé of a long experience.

Love devotedly the masters who preceded you.

Kneel before Phidias and Michelangelo. Admire the divine serenity of the one, the fierce anguish of the other. Admiration is a generous wine for noble spirits.

Guard yourself, however, in imitating your seniors. Respect tradition and search to discern what it encloses of eternity. Love nature and sincerity: They are the two strong passions of geniuses. All geniuses have adored nature and never have they lied. So tradition tends to you the key by which you will avoid the routine. It is tradition itself which bids you to relentlessly enquire for the truth, which forbids you from submitting blindly to each master.

So nature should be your unique goddess.

You should have in her an absolute faith. You should be certain that she is never ugly, and limit your ambition in order to be faithful to her.

All is beautiful for the artist; for in all beings and all things his search penetrates to discover the character, that is to say, the inner truth which hides under the form. And that truth is beauty itself. Study religiously. You cannot miss finding beauty, for you will meet truth.

Work tenaciously.

You, sculptors of statues, fortify in yourself the sense of depth. The mind does not easily grasp that notion. It images distinctly only surfaces. To imagine the forms in thickness is toilsome. However, that is your task.

Above all, you should establish distinctly the large planes of the figure that you sculpt. Accent vigorously the orientation that you give to each part of the body, the head, the shoulders, the pelvis, the legs. Art requires some decisions. It is by the well-accented flight of the lines that you plunge into space and give depth to your work. When your planes are fixed, all is found. Your statue lives already. The details are born and they are disposed of quickly by themselves.

When you model, never think of the surface but in relief. Your mind should conceive each surface form as the extremity of a volume that pushes itself from behind. Figure the forms as pointing at you. All life surges from a center. Then it germinates and opens up from within to the outside. The same in good sculpture; one feels always an impulsive pushing out from the interior. It is the secret of the antique.

You painters, observe the same reality in depth. Look, for example, on a portrait by Raphael. When that master represents the face of a person, he makes the chest recede obliquely and that is how he gives the illusion of the third dimension.

All the great painters sounded out space. It is in that notion of volume in depth that their force resides.

Remember this: There are no contours; there are only volumes. When you draw, never preoccupy yourself with contour but with relief. It is the relief that determines the contour.

Work without stopping. It is necessary for you to break yourself in thoroughly through your craft.

Art is nothing but feeling. But without the science of volumes, proportions, colors—without the dexterity of the hand—the most animated feeling is paralyzed. What will become of the greatest poet in a strange country of which he is ignorant of the language? In the new generation of artists there are numerous poets who, unfortunately, refuse to learn to speak. Thus they are only able to stutter.

Patience! Do not count on inspiration.

Inspiration does not exist. The only qualities of the artist are wisdom, attention, sincerity and will power. Accomplish your job as an honest worker.

Be truthful, young people. But that does not mean being dully exact. There is a low exactitude—that of the photograph and of the casting.

The artist who contents himself with his vision and reproduces subserviently the details without value will never be a master.

If you have visited cemeteries in Italy, undoubtedly you have remarked upon the childishness with which the artists charged to decorate the tomb attach themselves to the soul.

Nearly all our sculptors recall those of the Italian cemeteries.

In the monuments of our public places one distinguishes only frock-coats, tables, flags, chairs, machines, balloons and telegraphs. Have a horror of that rubbish. Know the interior truth, which represents the art. Art only begins with the true interior—when all your forms, all your colors translate the feelings.

Do not fear unjust criticism.

It will revolt your friends. It will force your friends to reflect sympathy when they will flock to you, and they will parade this unjust criticism more resolutely when they discern the better of the works.

If your conception is original, you will count at first only a few friends, and you will have a multitude of enemies. Do not be discouraged. The first will triumph, for they know why they like you; the others will ignore why you are hateful to them. The first are passionate for the truth, and will recruit incessantly new adherents. The others testify no durable zeal for their false opinions. The first are tenacious; the others turn with all the winds. **The victory of the truth is certain.**

Do not lose your time in gaining worldly or political relationships. You will see many of your colleagues arrive by intrigue to honor and fortune. They are not true artists. Some among them are, however, very intelligent, and if you attempt to fight with them on their ground you will consume as much time as they—that is to say, all your existence. Nothing remains for you but being an artist.

Love passionately your mission, for there is nothing more beautiful. It is much higher than the vulgar believe it is.

The artist is a great example.

He adores his work; the most precious compensation is the joy of doing well. Actually—alas!—people induce in the workers their misfortune to hate their work and botch it. People will be happy only when they will have the mind of the artist, that is to say, when they will take pleasure in their work.

Art is again a wonderful lesson in sincerity.

The truthful artist always expresses what he thinks at the risk of overthrowing all the established prejudices.

By doing so, he teaches his contemporaries to be free. Can you imagine what marvelous progress would suddenly be realized if the absolute truth reigned among men? Oh, how quickly society would get rid of some errors and ugliness that it has acknowledged, and with what rapidity our earth would become a Paradise.

Heading West

In 1951 Turner's classmate Dick White called with the sad news that his brother Steve, who had been Turner's roommate at West Point, had been seriously injured in the Korean War. It was a head wound, but the family couldn't find out how bad it was because they didn't yet know Steve's location. The Whites' father, a retired army colonel living in Austin, Texas, mounted a vigorous letter-writing campaign in search of Steve. Finally Herb heard from Dick that they had located Steve in the army hospital in Tokyo and that he was being sent to San Antonio.

When Steve arrived, Dick called Herb to ask if he would be willing to come to San Antonio. Steve was suffering from amnesia and was unable to speak. His family hoped Turner's visit would at least comfort Steve and perhaps help him recover his memory and speech. Turner of course agreed to come, and soon.

As Turner planned the trip south, he considered making other stops along the way. Coming from a family of builders, Turner had long admired the work of American architect Frank Lloyd Wright, who was gaining an international reputation. Indulging his curiosity, Turner decided to take a brief detour to visit Wright's Chicago studio, half-considering the possibility of arranging to study with the architect. After arriving at Wright's studio, however, Turner realized that studying with Wright was not for him. Although he would have loved the opportunity to learn from the innovative architect, he found the environment in the studio uncomfortably competitive, and anyway the waiting list for apprenticeships was far too long.

Turner continued on to San Antonio, looking forward to visiting Steve. When he entered the medical ward, he saw Steve at the far end of the room with a group of family members. When Steve saw Turner he raised himself up with the help of a hanging handle bar to give him a welcoming, groaning salute. When Turner came closer, Steve grabbed him by the front of the shirt, groaning incomprehensibly. Thinking that Steve was expressing how happy he was to see him, Turner was overwhelmed with emotion. Then he realized Steve was trying to tell him something: Turner was wearing the shirt White had left behind while visiting Turner at the Brackman summer school. Steve's memory had come back. Commenting on the

THE CITY OF DEL MAR IS BUILT ON A DENSELY WOODED SANDSTONE HILLSIDE WITH NARROW, WINDING STREETS OVERLOOKING THE PACIFIC OCEAN.

44

meeting, Steve's brother Bill reported, "Steve is okay, but I'm worried about Herb." Steve was later transferred to a hospital in Framingham, Massachusetts, a little more than 100 miles from New York, allowing Turner to make regular weekend visits to his friend.

Soon after Turner returned from Texas to Saranac Lake, William Distin, an architect with whom Turner was working, showed him a magazine article about Frank Lloyd Wright's son, John Lloyd Wright, who lived in Del Mar, California. After reading the article and seeing the younger Wright's designs, which were similar in principle to his father's, Turner was drawn to the younger Wright. He felt he could get the same kind of instruction he would have received at Frank Lloyd Wright's studio—without the uncomfortably competitive atmosphere he had noticed among the apprentices in Frank Lloyd Wright's studio, and without having to wait years for an opening.

When Turner told his parents he wanted to travel to Del Mar to study with Wright, his father advised him to send the architect a letter first. Turner disagreed—he wanted to drive out and show up at Wright's door, rationalizing that it would be harder for Wright to refuse him if he were to knock on his door with suitcase in hand. Before leaving for California, however, Turner did send a letter to Colonel White in Austin, asking if he could stop by and visit on his way out to Del Mar. After witnessing Colonel White's letter-writing campaign in search of his son, Turner figured White might know someone who could facilitate Turner's introduction to Wright. Sure enough, White knew Wright's sister, with whom he had been in a high school production of *The*

Pirates of Penzance. The colonel sent off a letter of introduction, but Turner didn't wait around for a potential "no." He headed for Del Mar, even as the letter saying Wright had accepted Turner was making its way back to Colonel White's house in Austin.

Turner arrived at John Lloyd Wright's doorstep on the first Sunday of October, 1952. When Wright's stylish wife Frances, with her short ruffled hair and dramatically painted eyes, opened the door, Turner's first feeling was trepidation. Frances was wearing a turquoise sweater, black-and-white checked pants, and Indian jewelry. Seeing someone made up in this fashion on a Sunday reminded Turner of his father's concern about Californians and movie stars. Casting his fears aside, though, Turner entered the house and was invited to speak with John Lloyd Wright. In the course of a long, nebulous conversation, Turner realized that Wright was planning to let him stay. Before the day was over, Turner moved into a studio apartment off Wright's office, for which he paid $35 a month, and began his three-year stint as Wright's apprentice.

DESIGNING
DEL MAR

With the journey to Del Mar, once again Turner's powerful instincts and stubborn determination had paid off. John Lloyd Wright was a practicing architect and a true pioneer, and he fit Turner's definition of a master. Turner had now established a new stage on which to act. In the fertile creative environment of the Del Mar region, working in Wright's own studio, he would begin the apprenticeship and the work that would define his career.

ONE OF HERB
TURNER'S CLASSIC DEL
MAR DESIGNS, BUILT
FOR THE VICE-
PRESIDENT OF THE
SAN DIEGO SIERRA
CLUB.

As a newcomer to Southern California, without friends or family in that part of the world, Turner found himself thrown back on his own resources. He was nevertheless determined to acquire the skills he would need in pursuit of an architectural career. His artistic ambitions aside, Turner also had an entrepreneurial streak, with an appreciation for business and finance that he had inherited from his parents. He would later combine these talents as a designer, builder, developer and real estate investor. His architectural practice would come to reflect the practical considerations that confronted him in the rough-and-tumble world of contracting and building. The speculative projects he would engage in would not always lead to successful outcomes, but Turner's uncompleted projects would suffer more from the lack of imagination of the various civic and political organizations he was forced to deal with than from a lack of understanding of the process on his part. He would often have to contend with reactionary forces in the communities with which he engaged who did not share his vision and his principles.

A born problem-solver with skills honed at West Point, and an artistic Renaissance man with passion and talent for painting, sculpture and architecture, Turner charted his own distinctive approach. During his career he has fashioned an unaffected architectural style in tune with leading trends in West Coast residential building, toward a kind of relaxed modernism. Stepping away from the severe minimalism of better-known practitioners of the day, this comfortable and livable approach to housing and commercial

JOHN LLOYD
WRIGHT'S HOME
STUDIO IN DEL MAR,
WHERE TURNER
APPRENTICED FOR
THREE YEARS.

THE WRIGHT LIVING
ROOM, WHERE THE
APPRENTICE TURNER
WAS WELCOMED AS A
MEMBER OF THE
FAMILY.

spaces was not radically different from what a number of other committed designers around him were trying to achieve. But it was exceptional in one regard: Turner had profound enthusiasm for the physical beauty of the region in which he found himself. Eventually he would consolidate his ideas on design and love of landscape into an overall philosophy that was uniquely his own. But at twenty-six, Turner, the newcomer in Del Mar, was poised for his next phase of learning and growth.

The Apprentice

John Lloyd Wright's split-level Del Mar house was built into a hill with the living area below and an efficiency apartment and studio/office above. Turner lived in the apartment, and early each morning he would open the office. Wright usually worked late, so he did not come upstairs to the studio until noon or so. He worked on business from noon to four p.m. and then on design until eight p.m. or later. Each night Wright would make corrections on the drawings Turner was working on, and each morning Turner would respond with revisions. Working in the studio, which overlooked the Wrights' living room, brought him into intimate contact with the family and their lively household. Turner, treated more as a family member than an employee, was invited down to dinner on occasion and to social events, where he was usually introduced as Wright's apprentice. He lived and worked under this arrangement with John Lloyd Wright for the next three years.

After explaining the finer points of his critique of Turner's work, Wright would turn to his own work while Turner unobtrusively observed his technique and style. To the young beginner, learning by example was the best training imaginable. He eagerly accompanied Wright on countless site visits and noted his every activity. On one such trip, a client was interested in how Wright instructed his apprentice. In response, Wright said, "I don't teach or instruct. His job is to observe."

Turner began to notice that continuity was central to Wright's aesthetic philosophy. By focusing on a single architectural element, Wright would create a visual theme and structural continuity in the design of a house. The fixed primary form would be modified based on the project's unique conditions and requirements, with details added to the frame like muscles on a skeleton. Such hallmarks of Wright's design clearly distinguished his work from that of other architects, but did not keep him from being compared to his famous father. Throughout his life, John had worked on many projects with Frank Lloyd Wright—from Midway Gardens in Chicago to the Imperial Hotel in Japan. Yet Wright had no desire to imitate his father, to become a better or worse version of the elder architect. John Lloyd Wright wanted to be John Lloyd Wright and strove to develop his own simple, practical, easy-to-build designs. To assist in the design visualization process, Wright developed a system of modular blocks that later came to be marketed as Wright Blocks, a product for both children and architects. Wright also made a mark in popular culture with Lincoln Logs, the building system he developed for children and which opened many a young mind to the possibilities of building and architecture.

Though both Frank Lloyd Wright and his scion, John, were great architects, unfortunately father and son were never really close. It has been said that Frank Lloyd Wright, a man whose only capacity for love and understanding seemed to be for architecture, has been called a "one-dimensional genius." Everything else, including family, was secondary. While working together in Tokyo on the Imperial Hotel from 1917 to 1922, the father and son had a falling out. Frank returned to the United States, leaving his son in Japan to continue working on the building. Sometime later, in an act that John considered to be only fair, he took part of a check he had been instructed to collect for his father. This incensed the elder Wright, and he fired John from the project. Later, though the two men tried hard to forge a strong relationship, sadly they never truly saw eye to eye again. While John's relations with his father foundered, his brother Lloyd maintained an on-and-off working relationship with Frank, probably because he was more inclined than John to stand up against his father's overbearing personality.

Independence

When Turner completed his apprenticeship with John Lloyd Wright, he found himself still craving more instruction in sculpture. He looked to his former instructor, Naum Los, for further guidance. Los had moved from New York to Florida and then to San Diego, but found the seaside climate unsatisfactory and soon relocated to Arizona. Turner urged his teacher to open another school, but Los was intent on retiring. When Turner was unable to find comparable education elsewhere in the area, his desire to continue sculpting ebbed. Years later, he found some satisfaction in a weekly live-model class with A. Wasil at the newly opened art studio of the Athenaeum Music and Arts Library in La Jolla, just south of Del Mar. Working with Wasil reinvigorated his desire to sculpt and stimulated his search to find instruction.

On a trip to the east coast, Turner visited the Lyme Academy, an art college with a contemporary focus on the traditions and history of representational art. There sculpture instructor Don Gale recommended him to Robert Cunningham, a Los Angeles sculptor. Turner promptly dove into intense study with Cunningham, leaving Del Mar at 7:30 a.m. to attend two classes, and returning to Del Mar about 1:00 a.m. This routine, on top of his already heavy schedule, led to a hospital stay in Los Angeles. But he was soon off to Loveland, Colorado, for a ten-day workshop with Don Gale. With his artistic passion satisfied, the entrepreneur in him kicked

in as he became involved with the Athenaeum School of the Arts and expanded it into the New School of Architecture. Both A. Wasil and Don Gale taught workshops there. He was getting closer to home.

In 1955 Turner briefly contemplated either going back to Saranac Lake in New York or moving elsewhere. But he decided to stay in Del Mar. Not only was he in love with the region, but he reasoned that if it was good enough for John Lloyd Wright, who had traveled widely and even lived abroad in Japan, then it was good enough for him.

TURNER'S FIRST REAL ESTATE DEVELOPMENT, HIS OWN HOUSE, BUILT ON "THE LEAST EXPENSIVE LOT IN THE BEST NEIGHBORHOOD."

53

Eager now to put down roots, Turner connected with a realtor who gave him some advice that he would later put to use in many of his projects: Find the cheapest (and usually the worst) lot in the best surroundings, and the good neighborhood will pull you up with it. Keeping that in mind, Turner purchased his own plot of land and built a studio with the proper northern exposure. His father gave him $7,500 to build the house, and he had someone else build the outer shell with the understanding that he would work out the interior himself. (For more about the evolution of the Turner house from 1956 to the present, see page 106.)

With his home established, Turner threw himself into his painting. In a short time he was participating in local exhibitions and winning awards. Soon he began giving painting lessons that proved to be highly lucrative

MASTERS AND TEACHERS: TURNER ON THE HERITAGE OF HIS IDEAS

The genealogy of the principles I have used in solving problems proceeds back in time from John Lloyd Wright through Frank Lloyd Wright, Louis Sullivan, and Eugene Emmanuel Viollet-le-Duc, the nineteenth-century French archeologist, theoretician, and teacher. I was independently introduced to the work of Horace Lecoq de Boisbaudran by Mr. Naum Los and to the work of Viollet-le-Duc by John Lloyd Wright. Mr. Los also introduced me to L. D. Luard's translation of Lecoq's *Training of the Memory in Art,* which I read with great enthusiasm.

It was a revelation to me when I realized that the two French contemporaries, Lecoq and Viollet-le-Duc, were the fountainhead from which issued the principles for both my painting and my architecture: I read in Luard's book: "Lecoq received open encouragement from Viollet-le-Duc, who strongly advocated the adoption of his [Lecoq's] methods in an article that he [Viollet-le-Duc] wrote condemning academic teachings of the day."

In the actual practice of sculpture and architecture, I have realized that there are certain universal artistic principles that apply to both art forms. As an architect, I had been interested in the work of Frank Lloyd Wright when I was a student in New York City. And following the advice of Mr. Los to study the teachers of my masters, I studied Wright's early work and soon discovered his *Lieber-Meister* (beloved master) was Louis Sullivan, and further that Sullivan, as a boy of nineteen years, had studied in Paris in the late 1800s, a creative period when two great masters were practicing their respective professions there: Lecoq de Boisbaudran in the training of visual arts and Viollet-le-Duc in his visionary theory of architecture. Also, Rodin, at that time was exhibiting his first major figure work, *The Age of Bronze.*

John Lloyd Wright's interest in the Viollet-le-Duc's work was firmly established when his father gave him a copy of Viollet-le-Duc's discourses, with the words, "In these volumes you will find all the architectural schooling you will ever need. What you cannot learn from them you can learn from me."

Viollet-le-Duc studied how and *why* buildings were built as they were, whereas most architects studied and copied the façades only. Viollet-le-Duc's approach to examining the underlying factors that inspired or required the resulting design solutions gave rise to two important principles in the development of architecture: Louis Sullivan's interpretation that "Form follows function" and Le Corbusier's maxim "A house is a machine for living in."

The primary inspiration for Sullivan's dictum came from his study of organic forms in the plant kingdom, leaves in particular. Frank and John Lloyd Wright would later use the term "organic architecture" to describe the design methodology that derived from Sullivan's approach.

Studying *Training of the Memory in Art* and experiencing the teachings of Mr. Naum Los Led me to recognize the distinct differences between studying with a "master" and studying with a "teacher": A master teaches by his work and a teacher by his instruction and his method. The great danger in studying with a master is that you become a weak imitation, or at best, a good imitation, because the acknowledged power of the master or his ideas becomes permanently implanted in your mind. A teacher, on the other hand, teaches you a method and cultivates a process for you to develop your own art form. Frank Lloyd Wright was a great master, but neither he nor anyone else has commended him as being a great teacher.

for the struggling young artist. Working with several students at once, he could earn as much as $45 per hour, a marked improvement over the $1.50 an hour he took home from drafting jobs.

During this time Turner met Marysa Senn, a figure model who posed for art classes in the San Diego area. They were married in 1958. Marysa continued modeling and Turner continued to do freelance architectural work and to teach. As his teaching reputation grew, he soon found himself devoting at least one full day and evening to it each week. At the same time, he decided to pursue his contractor's license and offer a combination "design-and-build" practice. His West Point degree qualified him to take a state licensing board exam. To learn the legal aspects of the business, he went to night school, then took the exam and became a contractor.

Hoping to further his experience as a designer, Turner went to work for Dale Nagel, a young architect who had recently graduated from the University of Southern California and relocated to San Diego to work with a contractor. Turner worked for Nagel three days a week for a little over a year. As he learned more about working drawings, post-and-beam construction and new tract-home techniques under Nagel, he was widely exposed to the local California architectural community, learning everything he could about the area and its architects in the process.

For an office, Nagel had rented a small room, little more than a walk-in closet with one window, in a small house near the beach. He and Turner shared the cramped little studio. Later, a contractor repaid a debt to Nagel by remodeling a larger office, where Turner continued to work, hanging his paintings in the front room. Soon Turner phased himself out of his employment with Nagel, which marked the last time that he would work for someone else. Dale Nagel later built up a large architecture practice.

When Turner attempted to become a licensed architect, however, he met with frustration. He was told by a dean of the University of Southern California that his West Point training would not count toward his architecture licensure, nor would his work with John Lloyd Wright. Since Turner knew he could still build houses as a contractor, he decided to begin a "design-and-build" practice. By partnering with licensed architect Don Cook, Turner was able to design and build a succession of small commercial and residential projects.

When Turner launched his career during the late 1950s, many of his clients were struggling to make ends meet. He prided himself on making accurate estimates for attractive homes that could be built without breaking budgets. He charged $100 per page for his original plans (a bargain even in those impecunious times), half of which went to his partner, Cook. As his reputation for cost consciousness grew, Turner began to attract clients who appreciated such integrity: young professionals without much money who nevertheless wanted nice homes. Some of Turner's clients at this time were veterans from World War II who came to him through Cal Vet, a program that provided bank loans for veterans to build homes.

Acting as both designer and builder, Turner was able to control all the details of his projects, therefore guaranteeing budgets and timelines. He also provided his clients with a lot of flexibility in the design and budgeting process, because he could accurately predict the relative costs of different design solutions. He kept his budgets low and stayed within them. Because he knew how to optimize economic value in the building process, he developed a reputation for high-quality building on a budget. Although he had a steady flow of clients for his own projects, he soon began supplementing his income by building projects for other architects as well. Turner noted to his satisfaction that competing bids on these various architectural jobs were significantly higher than were his own. He was so highly regarded by the architects whose projects he built that they frequently hired him to build their own homes.

Contemporary Influences

Though their style often differed from his own, Turner appreciated the work of a growing number of architects of his time, who after World War II were deeply influenced by Japanese culture and aesthetics. Ironically, most architects had become accustomed to thinking of the Japanese not as former enemies, but as ambassadors of a new style. For example, Gordon Drake, an instructor at the University of Southern California, was stationed at various places around the Pacific Rim in the U. S. Marines during the war, and wrote memorably about the different styles he saw there. Pacific Rim culture would continue to influence California culture throughout the 1950s. Wooden post-and-beam construction, an integral part of the region's structures, became enormously popular on American shores, and wood replaced stucco as the building material of choice both inside and out.

This architectural impulse soon hit the mainstream, especially in Southern California. Most people at the time (many of whom, like Turner's own clients, were recently discharged soldiers) simply wanted a straightforward tract house built or purchased with a federal GI loan. Developers bought up parcels of land all over Orange County to accommodate them, usually from orchard farmers who had spent their lives farming the land and happily sold their property when they were ready to retire.

 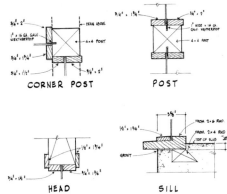

USING POST-AND-BEAM CONSTRUCTION, NEW INEXPENSIVE MATERIALS AND DISTINCTIVE CONTEMPORARY DESIGNS, SAN FRANCISCO DEVELOPER JOSEPH EICHLER, WHO WAS INSPIRED BY FRANK LLOYD WRIGHT, OFFERED HIGH-QUALITY ARCHITEC-TURE AT AFFORDABLE PRICES IN HIS DEVELOPMENTS.

Due to the sharp increase in demand for housing, the domestic building industry swiftly turned from the accepted practice of crafting individual homes to one of manufacturing houses by the hundreds, even thousands, based on a single "cookie-cutter" blueprint. As a result, homes became much more affordable, if less differentiated, in the post-war era.

In the architecture schools, students were excited that they could be designing homes of architectural distinction for thousands of people. However, once tract homes really caught on, those creative aspirations failed to come to fruition. The mass-production paradigm grew farther away from the established tradition of custom-built homes with individualized design and high-quality craftsmanship.

One builder who proved to be an exception to this trend was Joseph Eichler of San Francisco. A developer who had once lived in a Frank Lloyd Wright home himself, Eichler sought to make this kind of high-quality architecture available to the masses. To do so, Eichler hired some of the best young architects of the time, whose work embodied the open-space floor plans characteristic of his own designs. He also utilized new materials, such as inexpensive plywood from Japan, and introduced a host of details that would reduce costs while enhancing the style of his modest but highly livable houses. In a competitive market, Eichler was able to produce attractive buildings as cheaply as tract-home designers could.

Gradually, however, building codes changed in such a way as to preclude many of Eichler's economical design innovations. Eventually, post-and-beam construction was simply no longer allowed under the building code. To complicate matters, the popularity of Japanese plywood sent prices for the material through the roof. When Eichler tried to construct a different type of building (in one case, a condominium-style multiple housing development), expenses soared unexpectedly and in the process the developer went broke. Mindful of Eichler's experience, Turner realized that to pursue larger-scale developments, he would have to be far more creative to maintain his high standards in a business climate that was resolutely dedicated to keeping costs to the minimum.

Parallel Artistic Pursuits

When Turner had relocated from New York to California in 1952, he had left behind a large community of fellow Realist painters. During the years he had worked as a builder in California, he had grown out of touch with the New York art community. To bridge his past and present, and to expose Del Mar and the rest of the San Diego community to significantly higher-quality painting technique and Realist expression, Turner began planning an exhibition of work by nationally recognized Realist artists, called *20th Century Realists*.

At the time, the fashionable movement in painting was Abstract Expressionism, a style that Turner judged to be inherently flawed. To appreciate this form of art, he reasoned, the viewer was required to intuitively think like the artist and understand his emotional makeup. Turner, a Realist himself, naturally preferred the work of painters who depicted more tangible subjects and relied on techniques, skill and original ideas to show the human condition.

EXPLORING HUMAN POTENTIAL

In the late 1960s and early 1970s the Human Potential movement spilled out across America, influencing hundreds of thousands of people. The San Diego area was home to many of the movement's innovators, and was considered one of the leading "markets" for the new personal-growth disciplines. While the movement addressed various aspects of human potential in the realms of "body, mind and spirit," at the time it was best known for three main institutions: Transactional Analysis (TA), Transcendental Meditation (TM) and Erhard Seminars Training (EST).

Eric Berne's *Games People Play: The Psychology of Human Relationships* introduced the concept of Transactional Analysis to a wider audience, while Thomas Anthony Harris's *I'm OK, You're OK* expanded on the concept, bringing TA more prominently into the public eye. At about the same time, the principles in Maharishi Mahesh Yogi's newly published *Science of Being and Art of Living: Transcendental Meditation* helped to popularize that movement, along with Harold Bloomfield's *TM: Discovering Inner Energy and Overcoming Stress.* Turner, who often encountered Dr. Bloomfield during early-morning walks along the beach, became actively interested in both TM and TA, but he ultimately focused on the third approach— EST, the developmental techniques devised by Werner Erhard. EST aimed to provide individuals and organizations with a means by which they could think more creatively and independently and bring about real change in their lives. An enormously popular move-ment, EST attracted approximately a million adherents between 1971 and 1981, who flocked to Erhard's seminars, making his methodology a household word at the time.

In the same manner that Turner was influenced by the training in self-discipline and integrity he received at West Point, he responded to the core concepts of EST—transformation, integrity and language—and, to his excitement, the positive changes he'd seen in others who had taken the training. Turner enrolled in a series of seminars and workshops, interested in seeing how the principles of EST would manifest in real life. For Turner, the EST experience provided a safe space for questioning, expressing and sharing, always with the explicit understanding that students would take what they learned within EST and use their discoveries in the larger context of the outside world.

Transformation using Erhard's principles was not easy, nor were the seminars inexpensive. However, Turner believes he benefited greatly from studying EST's principles of integrity and transformation, learning to take risks that would produce extraordinary results.

A few years after beginning work in Erhard's program, Turner leapt into the purchase of a 232-acre mountain property in nearby Escondido, California, that happened to remind him of his youthful surroundings in the Adirondacks. A short time later, he took another chance and bought a 10,000-acre ranch in the state of Oregon, trading shares in his proposed Southfair two-acre commercial center in Del Mar as part of the deal. While Turner originally had no idea how to approach either development project, his risk-taking eventually paid off. Not only was he putting his EST training to work, but he was learning in new areas and undertaking new challenges.

During World War II, many of the contemporary American Realists served in the military in some capacity, while Nelson Rockefeller and oth-ers at the Museum of Modern Art, supported by an intellectual elite, strove to associate themselves with new forms of European and American art. Good Realist painting exhibitions were hard to come by, not only elsewhere but especially on the West Coast. Turner decided he wanted to organize a show in Realist art in his vicinity so that people could at least compare the two movements of Abstract Expressionism and Realism. Turner, with other fellow artists, notably Donal Hord (a sculptor), and Roy Mason (a watercolorist) invited artists on both the East Coast and the West Coast to submit to the show, whether they knew them or not. To their amazement, a large number submitted. These artists, whose work was then considered to be out of fashion, were clearly delighted to have their work displayed. One such artist was Peter Hurd, who had also attended West Point, had married the sister of Andrew Wyeth and had introduced Wyeth to egg tempera painting, a rarely used and very old technique, which Turner later adopted.

It was a very successful show, and the group's subsequent exhibits were even more so. The artists appreciated that someone was showing their work and understood that California was a great new venue to show their art. The shows were noticed in New York as well, where galleries couldn't even get the same artists to speak to one another, let alone exhibit together. By the time he closed the sixth show, Turner figured he had gained what he wanted out of exhibiting: new techniques and above all, new artistic concepts.

CATALOG FOR THE *20TH CENTURY REALISTS* EXHIBITION ORGANIZED BY TURNER AT THE SAN DIEGO ART INSTITUTE IN 1960.

The Sea Ranch Inspiration

Like those of many of his architectural peers, Turner's ideas about residential design were indelibly marked by the development of the Sea Ranch, the mid-1960s multi-residential complex on the coast of northern California designed by the San Francisco Bay Area architectural firms Joseph Esherick and Associates, and Moore, Lyndon, Turnbull and Whitaker (MLTW), and land planners Lawrence Halprin and Associates. Set in pristine surroundings, the Sea Ranch, with its intimate groupings and dramatic forms, paid respectful tribute to the landscape and vernacular

TWO PAINTINGS
FROM THE *20TH
CENTURY REALIST*
SHOW AT THE SAN
DIEGO MUSEUM OF
ART, BY TEXAN PETER
HURD, WHO PAINTED
IN EGG TEMPERA
(TOP), AND BY NEW
YORK OIL PAINTER
JOHN KOCH
(BOTTOM).

61

buildings of the region. Although compromised in later years by further development that substituted oversized single-family dwellings for condominiums, the Sea Ranch was the model for a torrent of imitative structures in uninspired settings that rarely rose to match MLTW's startling achievement. For himself, Turner absorbed the lessons of Sea Ranch and sought to incorporate them into his practice.

Turner followed the project closely as it was covered extensively in *Sunset* magazine and visited the Sea Ranch several times. Typical of his approach to learning from professionals he respected, Turner became acquainted with Al Boeke, the primary visionary and driver of the Sea Ranch. The sprawling community was undoubtedly a key inspiration for Turner: The sensitive land planning by Lawrence Halprin sowed the seeds for the "terramonic" design philosophy that Turner was to adopt later (see page 95); and the organic-modern architectural style, with natural woods, clean lines, large windows, high ceilings and interior-exterior connections greatly influenced Turner's own architectural contributions to Del Mar.

The Sea Ranch was essentially conceived as a grouping of vacation homes, while Turner was building for clients who were making his houses their homes. Also, the Sea Ranch had the distinct advantage of being built far away from surrounding development. Turner, for his part, was operating in a semi-rustic but nevertheless urbanized environment subject to restrictions dictated by traffic arteries, adjoining structures and related complications. He was also distinctly aware of contemporary stylistic influences that dictated innovative design features such as visual pathways, which connected relatively confined street views with panoramic vistas.

Working on what are by today's bloated standards relatively tiny buildings, Turner strove to accommodate the demands of married couples with growing families, who also needed their privacy. His floor plans tended to minimize the square footage of circulation areas, particularly critical when space was at a premium, and to separate public areas—living, dining and kitchen—from sleeping areas that further respected the division between parents and children. In step with sweeping societal changes that encouraged the growth of extended families, these segregated areas would later serve admirably the needs of "empty nesters" whose grown children would later return for visits with families of their own.

AL BOEKE ON THE SEA RANCH

In a free-enterprise society, good things happen along with the bad, but most outcomes—compromised by the misguided efforts of the ignorant or incompetent—fall somewhere in between. In the case of intentionally designed communities, the time it takes to develop a structure according to a master plan invites unanticipated intrusions beyond the creator's control. When unused or cultivated land is converted to house a growing population, there is an inherent opportunity to profit, but for those with an environmental vision, there is also an incentive for real excellence.

Sufficient examples exist today to prove that land development can be orderly, profitable and sustaining for its owners, and that the notion of excellence can lead to beauty, economy, sustainability, humanity and even good architecture. Historically, however, relatively few advanced community developments following ecological principles in their approach have had the luxury of supervision by local government, builders and consultants who have the vision, desire and organization to achieve this degree of viability.

Whether a condominium, a farm enclave, or a collection of a dozen houses around a cul-de-sac, a well-designed development with "green" sensibilities can attract and sustain families in a sympathetic, creatively integrated community. However, this process requires extraordinary incentives involving community design, architecture, ecology, law, scheduling and economics, public relations, marketing and of course, government. Meanwhile the much-maligned developer must share those incentives while having a strong financial support to weather the vagaries of the economy and unforeseen political machinations. The latter, especially, can neither be anticipated nor controlled, nor can politicians be expected to share the developer's vision. Without the requisite education and training, the public themselves will not be much help either.

Given the pace and scale of normal development in the United States, the ideal of an expansive, sustainable community, to say nothing of significant architecture, seldom happens, but the good news is that it has, it does, and it can.

Al Boeke was the primary designer of the Sea Ranch development. For more on the Sea Ranch, see the Epilogue, "Toward a Greener Future."

THE SEA RANCH, BUILT IN THE 1960S ON THE NORTHERN CALIFORNIA COAST, FOLLOWING THE ECOLOGICAL DESIGN VISION OF ARCHITECT-DEVELOPER AL BOEKE AND A CIRCLE OF INNOVATIVE ARCHITECTS AND LAND PLANNERS, WAS A PROFOUND INFLUENCE ON TURNER AND HELPED INSPIRE HIS "TERRAMONIC" DESIGN PHILOSOPHY.

A Selection of Commercial and Residential Projects

Turner's architectural work evolved through the 1960s and '70s as a series of custom home projects and innovative commercial developments. Several of these projects are presented here in brief, followed by more extensive descriptions of Southfair, perhaps Turner's best-known commercial project, and the Turner residence, which evolved from his original Del Mar studio and has remained his family's home to present. Project locations are shown on a map on page 114.

A CHARACTERISTIC TURNER ENTRANCE TO THE SOUTHWORTH RESIDENCE, FEATURING SEAMLESS INDOOR-OUTDOOR CONNECTION.

SOUTHWORTH RESIDENCE FLOOR PLAN AND INTERIOR.

SOUTHWORTH RESIDENCE (1963)

The Southworths bought a 50 x 100 ft. flat lot that they felt had no redeeming characteristics whatsoever, aside from its affordability. They asked Turner if he would be interested in developing it. Turner replied, "If it's legal and it's cheap, it's a great lot." The lot was flat and was bordered by the back sides of two fences; it had no off-site view or other amenities, so any interest had to be created inside the lot.

Turner's concept used the walls of the house as the enclosure, directing all activities inward. Also, the house was divided into two zones, one for

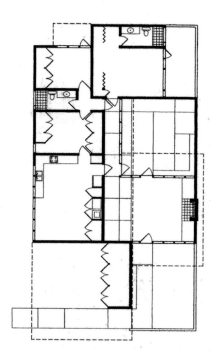

adults and the other for family. The adult space comprised an entry court, a living–dining room enclosed on two sides by high glass walls, and a patio. This combination of transparent open space enclosed by solid walls and high ceilings created an interesting contrast of open and closed spaces. The family room area was a continuous series of spaces: family room–kitchen, bath and bedroom connected by a linear traffic pattern. An article on the Southworth house was published in the "Home" section of the *Los Angeles Times*.

MATHES RESIDENCE (1966)

Since 1935 Bob and Ruth Mathes from New Jersey had been building a structure that they had continued to add onto during their summer visits to California. It was a very warm and comfortable living environment but too small and uncoordinated.

The Matheses had been good friends of Turner's for years and had enthusiastically supported his painting. So when they turned to Turner for help in their home, Turner expressed concern that extensive work in designing and building it might adversely affect their relationship. Bob answered the question by asking one: "You mean that I can't have my home?"

That resolved Turner's doubts and he proceeded with the design. The Matheses had bought the site because it had a Mediterranean climate, which suited their Mediterranean art and furniture collections. Turner conceived a unique design for them, with a physical form in accordance with their Mediterranean taste and the Californian–Mediterranean climate. The design concept was a straightforward blending of California and Mediterranean architecture without any stylization, and the house was sited where the building would least disturb the land.

As the approach to the house, an entry bridge joins the carport to the front door. Immediately upon entering the house, the visitor is greeted with a sweeping view of the surrounding valley, created by glass walls that demarcate an inviting deck that floats over the panoramic countryside. The entryway leads directly into the living room–library, providing floor-to-ceiling bookcases, a fireplace and glass walls to the deck. To the right, the dining room, with its antique furniture and works of art, includes another glass wall opening out to the deck.

66

EXTERIOR OF THE MATHES RESIDENCE, SITUATED WITHIN THEIR EXISTING AVOCADO GROVE.

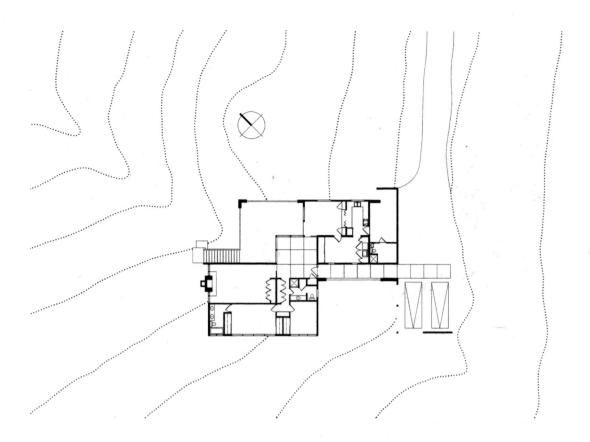

HELLEN RESIDENCE (1966)

Turner had earlier bid on the construction of a house for local resident John Hellen, designed by one of the area's most prominent architects, but the cost of the lot and the house proved to be too high and the project was abandoned. Hellen subsequently approached Turner about finding an inexpensive property in Del Mar with an ocean view where he could design and build a house. Turner located a long, narrow lot divided by a steep cliff. There were no views at the high ground level, but Turner conceived a design that extended the living area over the cliff on the property to allow for ocean views.

The completed design featured three distinct, cubic volumes distributed across the length of the property, the first for the garage, the second for the bedroom area and the third for the living room. The entrance, between the bedroom and the living room, was accentuated by two glass walls that provided an additional space on either side of the entrance.

Making the roof parallel with the structure's forms, Turner devised a square plan for the living room, dining area and kitchen that pushed the living room out above the cliff for the promised ocean view. He also covered this living space with a domelike ceiling.

THE HELLEN RESIDENCE: AN INEXPENSIVE LOT WITH A VIEW OF THE OCEAN MADE POSSIBLE BY TURNER'S DESIGN SOLUTIONS.

BERKICH RESIDENCE (1969)

Faced with designing a modestly priced home within a tight budget for George and Marge Berkich, Turner persuaded his clients to purchase an inexpensive, smallish lot that lay in a drainage pit and was surrounded on three sides by roadways.

Because storm water runoff was often trapped on the site, Turner raised the living area over a garage underneath. This not only reduced the ground coverage but also kept habitable quarters free of dampness and allowed for future additions at the garage level. His plan also provided a broad ditch to drain water off the site.

The adjacent streets that formed a half ellipse around the south, east and north sides of the property were connected on the west by a line of trees. To shield the building from the road, Turner created a protective shell of windowless walls around the perimeter, with the house opening to the west, and an entry court and views through trees to the ocean. The

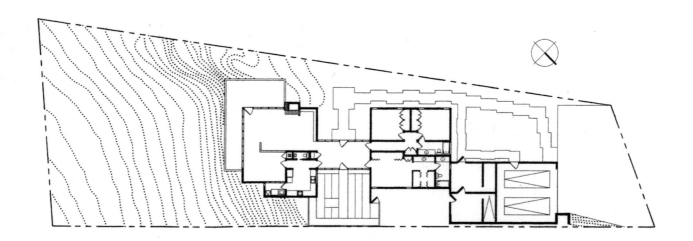

THE HELLEN RESIDENCE
ENTRY, CONNECTING THE
LIVING ROOM AND
BEDROOMS WITH AN
EXTERIOR PATIO.

THE "DOME CEILING," LIKE
MANY OF TURNER'S
INNOVATIONS, REQUIRED
UNCONVENTIONAL
CONSTRUCTION
SOLUTIONS.

A CANTILEVERED DECK
FACILITATES AN EXPANSIVE
OCEAN VIEW, WHILE ALSO
INTERACTING WITH THE
SURROUNDING HILLSIDE.

THE BERKICH
RESIDENCE LOT WAS
DENSE WITH TREES.
TURNER'S SITING AND
ARCHITECTURE
INTEGRATED THEM
INTO THE OVERALL
DESIGN, EVEN
RETAINING ONE
MAJESTIC TREE VIA A
STRATEGICALLY
PLACED OPENING IN
THE EXPANSIVE ENTRY
DECK.

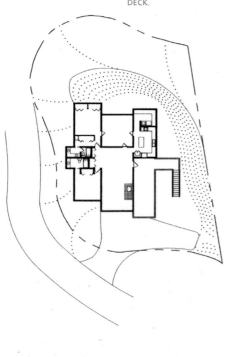

layout includes an enclosed "warm" deck to the south and an open but protected "cool" deck on the entry to the west.

Once again, the design of the house reconciled the demands of the owners' living needs with the challenges of a difficult site. As he likes to do in all his residential projects, in his layout Turner further economized on space by developing an efficient traffic pattern that eliminated hallways. Spaciousness in the small house was further enhanced by the maximum use of glass walls that led to exterior private decks.

RYPINSKI RESIDENCE (1970)

Richard and Carol Rypinski had purchased two forested lots in a secluded canyon behind a large historical Del Mar home. A city council member, Dick Rypinski was also a former president of the San Diego chapter of

THE RYPINSKI
HOUSE, DESIGNED
FOR ANOTHER
TREE-DENSE
SETTING, OFFERS
THE FEELING OF A
MOUNTAIN
CABIN, THOUGH
THE CENTRAL
VILLAGE OF DEL
MAR IS VERY
CLOSE BY.

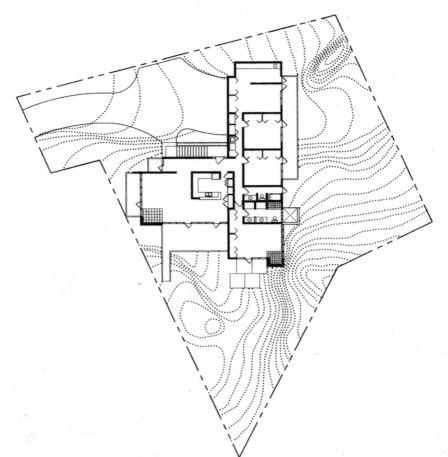

THE RYPINSKI LIVING
ROOM OVERLOOKING
THE DECK.

the Sierra Club and an early leader of the local environmental movement. Impressed with Turner's growing reputation for getting his designs built and staying within budget, Rypinski approached him with a model of the site, which he had studied closely, along with a notebook full of drawings describing all the rooms of the house and their function. He also informed Turner of his decision that none of the trees on the property were to be removed.

Turner's solution (to yet another challenging setting) was to design the building so the carport and the living area were situated on a lower and higher level respectively. The structure of the house was determined by vertical glass walls that provided views of the lot's forestation, along with slanted glass walls above the vertical glazing in the style of a painting studio that captured light from the sky through the foliage of the trees. Living room, kitchen and dining room faced onto a deck that also connected to the master bedroom and faced the treed south portion of the lot. The children's bedrooms faced east, separated from the adults' area by their orientation to an east-facing deck.

The Rypinski house offers the feeling of a remote mountain cabin, though the center of Del Mar village is just a four-minute walk away. Over 35 years later, this combination of rustic warmth and seclusion with immediate access to a vital community still provides the homeowners with a uniquely satisfying lifestyle.

NINTH STREET DEVELOPMENT (1971)

Turner was developing a busy residential practice, but building on a contract-by-contract basis proved frustrating. With no control over the flow of incoming work, he often found himself in the position of having either too much or too little to do. If the former, he often missed opportunities to bid on jobs he wanted, and if too little, he would have to take anything he could get. In order to mitigate the drastic fluctuations in his workload, Turner decided to buy property himself so that he would have some control over the designing and building schedules for the houses he would build there.

Developing housing for public consumption had the advantages of providing three "profit centers": in the purchase and sale of land, the creation

THE NINTH STREET
DEVELOPMENT
INCLUDED THREE
SINGLE-FAMILY
HOMES. TYPICAL
TURNER DESIGN
ELEMENTS INCLUDED
HIGH AND LOW
CEILINGS, INDOOR-
OUTDOOR
INTEGRATION VIA
WALL-SIZED
WINDOWS, AND
CONTRASTING
VERTICAL AND
HORIZONTAL SPACES.

of the design, and the building itself. Such an approach, Turner reasoned, if properly executed, would return a reasonable profit for the risk involved, and provide a steadier workload.

Turner began with the purchase of a single property with an option to later purchase two adjoining lots. The site was similar to that of the Southworth residence, which Turner had designed and built in 1963 (see page 64).

So-called "zero lot" subdivision layouts, in which the houses are built right up to the property lines, with no setbacks, had become popular around this time because they gave builders added width to work with as long as the facing walls of adjoining houses had no door or window openings. However, in this project the narrow 50-foot widths of the lots had already been established about 100 years earlier and the lot lines couldn't be altered. Turner thought he could still make the plan work. He came up with another approach, requesting a specific usage easement on each side of each lot, which would be left unchanged. The title company agreed, and he had his zero-lot usage without the need of a government ordinance. Turner again received media attention for his design when this project was featured in *Sunset* magazine.

PARK PLACE DEVELOPMENT (1972–1973)

Turner's next speculative effort, Park Place, was more ambitious. A landmark development in the Del Mar region, the project combined many design and development innovations, and further established Turner as an environmentally sensitive architect long before the concept of "green architecture" became fashionable.

Turner recognized the stunningly beautiful but challenging terrain of the site. The Park Place development was composed of nine lots and two half-lots with a dividing alley, rising steeply uphill from the west to the east, with a cliff running diagonally from the southwest to the northeast.

PARK PLACE, A TEN-
UNIT RESIDENTIAL
COMPLEX, WAS SITED
TO PRESERVE THE
CLIFFS, RATHER THAN
GRADING THEM
AWAY. STRATEGIC
OPEN SPACE BETWEEN
THE HOUSES AND
VERTICAL SEPARATION
WOULD PROVIDE
OPTIMAL VIEWS AS
WELL AS PRIVACY.

Turner's plan was to create what felt like a private 25,000–square foot park for a site that had originally been divided some 100 years prior. His design, which would give the individual residences a parklike setting and a sense of place, gave rise to the name Park Place.

The Park Place site included a dramatic sandstone bluff, characteristic of the region, that Turner was determined to preserve, long before bluff preservation became a key environmental issue in the area. Given Southern California's sensitive and delicate natural environment, Turner also wanted to preserve any existing native plants. Although there was no particularly striking vegetation on the site, whatever grew there was protected and nurtured.

Before he actually began a title search, Turner developed a preliminary plan that left the land in its natural state without disturbing the existing cliff, preserving it as open space controlled by the homeowners' association. The resulting layout created nine narrow, deep lots and by vacating the alley, a wide, shallow tenth lot from the two remaining half-lots.

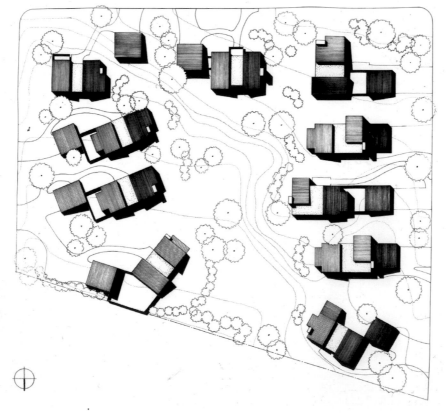

THE AWARD-WINNING
PARK PLACE PLAN DID
AWAY WITH THE
GRADING AND
FENCING OF SEPARATE
LOTS, POSITIONING
THE HOMES FOR
MORE OPEN SPACE
BETWEEN THE UNITS.
TURNER NEGOTIATED
WITH THE CITY OF DEL
MAR TO ELIMINATE
THE STANDARD ALLEY
THAT WOULD
TYPICALLY HAVE BEEN
REQUIRED BEHIND
THE HOMES, FURTHER
PRESERVING THE
NATURAL LANDSCAPE.

The nine houses on corresponding lots were designed to be long and narrow, bringing living environments deep into the site alongside the property's open space while providing ample room between buildings. The layout provided homeowners privacy from the street and from their neighbors and further allowed for generous view corridors from the street.

Layouts of the houses followed basically the same plan: A family room opened to a yard or courtyard, and the living area had either ocean or park views. The master bedroom was over the living room and children's bedrooms, allowing for primary and secondary views respectively. The basic three bedroom design allowed for modular "plug-ins": an additional bedroom, a dining room or other space, which could be integrated into the basic design without appearing to be merely added on.

Turner gave the assembled homes a common exterior design consisting of untreated cedar shingles that would be allowed to weather naturally to blend in with the natural vegetation. In siting the houses, Turner created open space while still allowing for privacy from traffic routes and adjoining neighbors. The long, narrow lots were perpendicular to the street, and the single wide, shallow lot was parallel to the street. On long and narrow lots, he eliminated windows on the long sides of the house and concentrated glassed areas on the narrow park-oriented side. In this way he was able to create neutral open space between adjoining houses while also shielding the home and its occupants from what were often busy thoroughfares. With these design solutions, he sought to achieve a unified but flexible architectural vocabulary that fostered a sense of place.

Park Place was entered into the American Institute of Architects' *Sunset Magazine* 1973–1974 Western Homes competition and received a citation award. The project was also featured in *House Beautiful*. With the success of the Park Place project, Turner thought he had found his niche, designing homes for a young, environmentally conscious new market. He looked forward to an exciting and successful future. The reality, as he discovered over time, was not quite what he had expected.

COAST DEL MAR CONDOMINIUM (1974)

Turner had just completed the ten single-family units of Park Place when he went on to his next development, a ten-unit condominium for a client in Del Mar. Most condominiums at the time were massive and continuous, with tenant parking under each unit.

Because of the small size of this lot, Turner decided to solve the parking problem by building the parking underground to leave more room for open space and living areas. To break up the mass of the building, he designed five duplex units and a pool, providing an experience close to that of single family residences, with private walls separating each unit from its neighbors. The residences in this project had a floor plan similar to that of Park Place, following its success in creating maximum usable square footage and volume.

COAST DEL MAR:
THE DAWN OF THE
CONDOMINIUM ERA,
DEL MAR STYLE, WITH
AN UNDERGROUND
PARKING GARAGE
THAT SAVED ROOM
FOR OPEN SPACE
ABOVE IT.

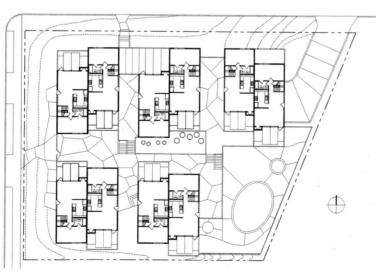

VILLAGE FAIR (1972–1980)

The Village Fair project entailed the adaptive reuse of a sixty-five-year-old garage, which mimicked the English Tudor style of the original and famous Del Mar Hotel. The garage's architecture was also consistent with the prevalent architectural style of Del Mar's commercial district, and sustaining it was important both for its continued use and for historic preservation of that style.

The structure of the garage portion of the building consisted of large bowstring trusses obscured by decades of paint layers, which were removed by sandblasting to impart a distinctive texture. A small apartment on the second floor was removed, and the floor was extended to the full width of the garage to provide an office for Turner and his associates. Low partitions divided this office, to preserve the open feeling of the restoration.

The renovated ground floor was separated down the middle by a passageway flanked by partial walls that stopped at five feet in height (so by code they were not walls), allowing for the complete visual opening up of the space.

McCamey Residence (1975)

The property was a small lot that was surrounded by streets on three sides, but it had an unobstructed view of the ocean, and its original soil was remarkably undisturbed. It was a modest property but the McCameys' demands were modest as well—a kitchen-dining-living room suite and a separate bedroom and bath. The site was the opposite of the Berkich house, located one block away (see page 68). Instead of being in a depression, it was on a hill with dense waterless soil without vegetation, so the house would be highly visible but the site had great potential for ocean views.

The house design was a solution of opposites: transparency for ocean views, opaqueness for privacy, small rafters for a delicate house with large exterior beams, and views to the west required in every room, for there were no views to the east.

THE MCCAMEY RESIDENCE, BUILT ON A VERY SMALL LOT SURROUNDED BY STREETS ON THREE SIDES, REQUIRED A DESIGN THAT PROVIDED OCEAN VIEWS FOR ALL ROOMS ON THE WEST-FACING EXTERIOR AND MAXIMIZED PRIVACY WITH WINDOWLESS WALLS ON THE STREET-FACING SIDES.

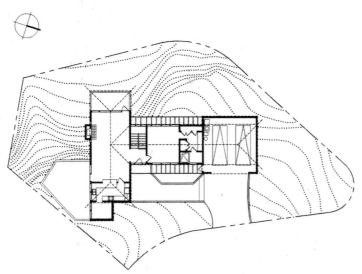

The kitchen, dining room and living room were in line, with a view to the ocean. The master bedroom had views to the west and glass walls to the east into an enclosed courtyard. Large ridge beams (structural elements) that were north-and-south and east-and-west held up 4 x 6-inch rafters.

There was only one workable location for the garage, and that was the lowest part of the upper portion of the lot. This placement provided ease of access for the automobile and determined the level of the floor of the main part of the house. This design used up the entire site, except for a little valley under the building that left room for the second bedroom. "This was one of those sites that designed the plan of the house," Turner reflects. "All I had to do was figure it out." The plan touched every setback line on the site.

The 32-foot-long ridge in the living room would require a massive exterior beam, but Turner solved the structural problems outside of the house, positioning the large ridge beams over the exterior ridge lines. The exterior hipped rafters were pointed toward the ocean. This resulted in a distinct, strong structural element on the outside of the house and a delicate ceiling structure inside.

COWETT RESIDENCE (1977)

The Cowetts first approached Turner to look at a house in Del Mar to remodel. When they described what they desired, Turner's response was, "You can't get there from here."

Turner suggested they look for an inexpensive lot instead. When they replied that they had been looking through the papers and contacting

THE COWETT HOUSE, WITH ITS CANTILEVERED DECKS, WAS DESIGNED TO CASCADE DOWN THE STEEP SLOPE, NESTLING INTO A GROUP OF TORREY PINE TREES.

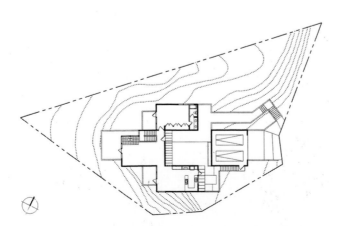

realtors for some time, Turner replied "You are looking at sellable lots ready to build upon. What you really need is a lot that's impossible to use in its present condition."

Fortunately, within a few weeks he found an oversized lot that the owners had tried to split but failed. Turner described a very simple solution and the Cowetts purchased the property.

The basic concept of this house was the cascading of the structure down a steep slope and the cantilevering of the decks and roof out into a group of Torrey Pine trees. The cascading started at the street with stairs leading to a bridge, leading to an enclosed courtyard, leading to the front door, which led to the entry for the living area and from there to the cantilevered decks and roofs that extended into the trees. Below this adult living area was the area for the children. The separation of the house into two distinct levels allowed for privacy and proved to be nicely adaptable to the needs of a growing family. Later, as the adults grew older, they didn't have to contend with the stairs, while their grown children, now with families of their own, always had a private place to stay when they came to visit.

Turner utilized an exposed 4 x 12-inch beam in a north-and-south direction to cantilever the roof and decks over the south exposure. This rigid construction allowed for a rafter ceiling without a ridge beam and posts for support.

This house has the suggestion of oriental architecture because Mrs. Cowett was of Chinese descent, and Turner knew that one of the principles of oriental building was the "continuity of construction." The repetition of the grammar of construction throughout the building contributed to a sense of relatedness and harmony among its spaces.

TORREY BLUFFS (1975–1977)

Turner's next project was sited on a three-and-a-half-acre parcel inside the San Diego city limits that bordered on Torrey Pines State Park and was surrounded on its other three sides by the streets of a neighborhood that had already been developed. The land was first offered to the state of California for park land, but the state refused to accept it. Turner knew that state law prohibited condemnation action for park purchase, so he felt his development project would be secure when he stepped in and purchased the property with a down payment; the seller was to carry the note. The project became for Turner the first of several lessons in the difficulties of dealing with local and state bureaucracies that often seemed intent on sabotaging his goals for the sites he developed.

Turner had come up with a proposal to develop twenty-five lots around the perimeter of the property, leaving roughly two acres of open space in the center that would also provide public access to the adjoining Torrey Pines Park. Stepping down into the canyon, each two-story house was laid out with the garage and living area at street level and the bedroom area below.

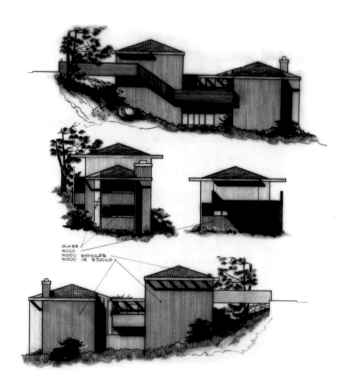

When he submitted the proposal to the city, some neighboring residents objected to certain aspects of the plan and began circulating petitions objecting to the project. This surprised Turner, who attempted to meet with the group but was thwarted by one member of the group, who did not want to give Turner the opportunity to meet his fellow petitioners, for fear that Turner's presentation might persuade them to withdraw their objections.

After two years of hearings, at a City of San Diego meeting to finally approve the project, state officials appeared. By means of a change in the law or an exemption, the state was, after all, condemning the property to acquire it for park purposes, partially to preserve its Torrey Pines. Once the state condemned the property, it had one year to finalize the condemnation. With characteristic tenacity, Turner filed suit alleging that the City of San Diego and the State of California were in collusion in delaying his project and bringing about the condemnation. During the resulting trial, the state was forced to defend itself by producing documentation that the City of San Diego had caused the continuing delays and to show reasons for every delay, in order to prove that the city was at fault for the delay and not the state. Turner had to prove that the city and state had colluded to deprive him of his property. Although he provided telling correspondence from the state to the city, the judge felt it was not enough evidence to find collusion. Turner did, however, get the City of San Diego's two-and-a-half years of delay before the jury.

The state eventually won what turned out to be an expensive decision, having to pay in excess of a half million dollars for a property that could originally have been purchased for a mere $55,000. Had the state not won, Turner's plan—for a property that itself included one sole living Torrey pine tree—would have provided access to Torrey Pines Park at no cost to the public, as well as two acres of open space.

Turner's Torrey Bluffs proposal did have positive, lasting consequences, however, that shaped future development in the area. When the City of San Diego adopted an ordinance regulating building on hillsides, Turner's designs were used as the model for hillside development.

BERNARDO MOUNTAIN (STARTED IN 1981)

Frustrated with his attempts to develop the Torrey Bluffs parcel, Turner took a plunge, using some of the proceeds of the condemnation of Torrey Bluffs to buy 232 acres of Bernardo Mountain in Escondido, for a sum somewhat in excess of $500,000 dollars. He had several reasons for the purchase. First, the parcel was a terrific bargain; second, the mountain bordered on Lake Hodges, stirring dreams he had had as a child of building in the Adirondacks. Also, Turner wanted to prove that there was a way that you could build successfully on hillside property, and there was no better hillside than a mountain. But perhaps just as important, this land, several miles north and east of Del Mar, was remote from the coastal zone,

TURNER PURCHASED THE SCENIC 232-ACRE BERNARDO MOUNTAIN PROPERTY IN 1981. HE DEVELOPED AN ECOLOGICALLY SENSITIVE LAND PLAN FOR THE SITE AND SPENT THE NEXT FIFTEEN YEARS SEEKING APPROVAL FROM THE COMMUNITY OF ESCONDIDO, BUT WITHOUT SUCCESS.

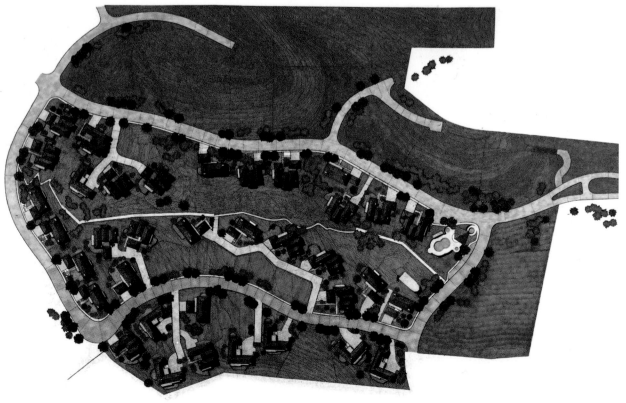

allowing him to avoid any further problems with the Coastal Commission. It was a project that he felt would be large enough to sustain him with continuous work and an established organization for some years to come.

Turner began thinking about the mountain property in the context of ideas he was developing that he termed *terramonics*, or building in harmony with the earth. He wanted to create a livable environment designed in such a way that the natural terrain was not interfered with, leaving the mountain largely intact, while designing his houses to fit into the existing landscape. Terramonics, then, is a method of addressing the concept of green architecture for human living by taking into consideration the relationship of the land to the house, a concern that even today, Turner believes, is largely ignored. In his view, contemporary discussion of green architecture primarily concerns the reuse of existing materials, the use of

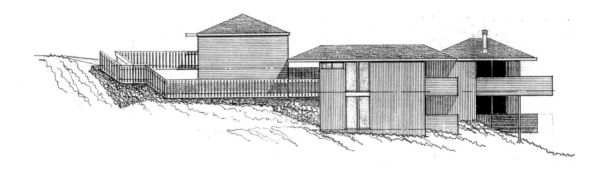

A TYPICAL ELEVATION FOR THE PROPOSED BERNARDO MOUNTAIN DEVELOPMENT.

environmentally friendly products in construction, and the choice of solar power, orienting the house toward the sun and so forth. When he began, Turner simply wanted to disturb the mountain he had purchased as little as possible. The mountain property included a small glen with room for 82 houses on 50 acres. Turner wanted to build there with a minimum of environmental impact.

An architect friend of Turner's advised him to talk to Joe Comella, an iconoclastic local land planner. Comella told Turner that he loved the concepts of Bernardo Mountain, but he tried to talk Turner out of developing the project because he felt the approval process would deaden Turner's new and creative ideas. Turner asked Comella pointedly, "Can it be done technically?" The answer was "yes." Turner went ahead and bought the property, and Comella came on board as the land planner.

THE TERRAMONIC SOLUTION

Herb Turner's architecture reflects a strong sense of regionalism, drawn partly from his love of nature, also reflected in his painting, and his love of place. His beliefs are exemplified by his *terramonic* design philosophy, which calls for building homes within natural landscapes with an emphasis on the interaction between interior and exterior spaces. Terramonics (his word) incorporates a number of key strategies that are too often insufficiently respected, or are even ignored altogether, in conventional architectural and planning practice.

Whether designing multiple dwellings or individual single-family homes, Turner's terramonic approach always begins with the site, striving to preserve as many of the features of the natural topography as possible. By minimizing grading, avoiding intrusive destructive concrete pads for foundations, and allowing the existing landforms to dictate the layouts of his plans, Turner has always tried to build in harmony with the terrain. Consistent with this approach, he has sought to provide parklike open spaces in the communal developments he has pursued. His landscaping has involved minimal interference with the existing ecosystem, with an emphasis on low-maintenance dry gardening that retains natural surface drainage.

But Turner was never a purist; his designs have often incorporated non-native but compatible species of plants to subtly modify and enhance the native vegetation. Custom plantings close to the house and in the interior allow for dramatic contrasts with the flora of the locale, providing another means of encouraging communication between indoors and outdoors.

While Turner's key strategy in designing homes has been to reflect and interact with the pristine natural landscape, other considerations regarding the site and the building's interior relationships are essential to a well-planned terramonic design. Turner feels that the experience of living in such a harmonious balance of nature and architecture can be likened to experiencing art, and that attention to how we live in the environment should be elevated to an art form. His designs nurture spatial relationships within the house itself that provide continuity with the exterior spaces. Entry areas allow for transitions to every zone of the house without spilling over into unrelated rooms. Where direct entry to each zone is not practical, traffic patterns are plotted so as not to interfere unduly with the use of each zone. Kitchens are grouped in an open plan with informal eating areas, and the family room is often adjacent to the more formal dining room. Both living room and family room are firmly oriented to the exterior by enclosed patios that open to the surrounding landscape features or ocean views. (For more on the terramonic approach, see the Epilogue, "Toward a Greener Future," starting on page 177.)

Comella saw land planning as a mathematical and visual art form, and he worked and lived his life as an eccentric artist. Passionate about his solutions, he would sometimes work without sleep for days. He was continually frustrated with the dogmatic community of civil engineers who were interested only in the sterile process of mass grading to produce the maximum number of flat pads for building units at the least cost.

In choosing Escondido for his next project Turner had assumed that the local residents would be easier to work with than those near Torrey Bluffs. But it soon became clear that the neighbors weren't going to make things easy for a newcomer they viewed as an outsider. Right away, a politically active local developer who was working on a property to the east managed to delay Turner from building on the mountain because it would interfere with the pristine views from his clients' sites.

Amid claims of collusion within the city government and changes in management, Turner was finally able to get the project approved by the city planning commission on its merits, then sent to the city council for final approval. It was finally approved by a three-to-two vote of the council, but the issue of sewers had not yet been resolved.

Meanwhile Turner was accumulating debt and interest on the project. Environment Now, an Orange County nonprofit organization dedicated to land preservation, loaned upwards of two million dollars to the project, with no direct involvement in the development process. Later, when their note came due at the time of the 1990s economic crash and the real-estate market collapse, no alternative potential lenders could be found for the project.

In the intervening years, moreover, all the low-lying land around the mountain had been bought up, so the property itself had become more valuable. Environment Now designed their own project for the mountain, using traditional flat pads, with a total of just 42 lots instead of the original 82, but at prices only the wealthy could afford. Although Turner subsequently found an amenable builder with an ample line of credit, his calls to the Environment Now organization were ignored. Environment Now had apparently decided that, rather than release the land back to Turner, it was better for their reputation to sell the land to a government agency for park purposes.

Turner worked on the Bernardo Mountain project for more than fifteen years, with his thinking fortified by his work with Al Boeke of the Sea Ranch and Frank Lloyd Wright's associate Aaron Green. Although much of the work involved solving a seemingly endless series of political and business challenges, it also provided a great deal of learning and inspiration about the potential for environmentally sound and economically sensible single-family-home developments. Turner is convinced, through his experiences with this project and others, that true "sustainability" requires, first and foremost, fully satisfied homeowners who will keep the home "in the family" and care for it over decades. Extend this principle to the community at large and the foundation is then established on which to build further sustainable features and designs.

THE COLONIAL INN (1977–1987)

A former hostelry, the 65-year-old Colonial Inn in the heart of La Jolla had been neglected for many years. Individual units were leased to elderly people who were willing to accept the Inn's rundown condition in return for very low rents.

The location of the building, its historical importance, and the quality of the original design argued for preserving it. Turner, with funds from Torrey Bluffs, purchased an interest in the property, along with an associate Bob Jones, an architect, and Don Emerson, a real estate entrepreneur. At the group's first meeting with a hotel consultant, they found themselves

THE COLONIAL INN RESTORATION WON AN AWARD FOR PRESERVATION, BUT TAUGHT TURNER AND HIS PARTNERS THAT THE HOTEL BUSINESS WAS NOT FOR THEM. THE HISTORIC BUILDING WAS SOLD TO A GROUP OF JAPANESE INVESTORS FOR SUBSTANTIAL PROFIT.

being lectured: "It is typical that people involved in building buy hotels because they think that the hotel building is the hotel business. It is not. The building is merely where the hotel business is carried on, and it is a business that the three of you know nothing about."

As it turned out, his warnings rang true as the three partners spent the next ten years learning more than they wanted to know about the hotel business. The project was a massive and continuous remodeling and refinancing process during that decade, and by its end the developers were ready to be out of the hotel business. Fortunately, at that time Japanese investors were interested in buying "trophy properties" in California, so it was sold in short order.

The Colonial Inn renovation won an award for preservation from the Save Our Heritage Organization (SOHO). With the sale of the property, the partnership made a substantial profit, proving to themselves that sustainability, in this sense by preserving and sustaining a classic building, can be financially rewarding.

POINT RANCH (1980)

At the turn of the decade, Turner acted on an offer he had received for a portion of the Southfair complex (described on page 100), with the proviso that the purchase would include swapping a property the buyer would purchase that Turner had long had his eye on. The property was Point Ranch, a working ranch of 10,000 acres on Goose Lake in Oregon on the California border that had been a money-losing operation as a ranch.

Turner started the process of planning the development with Al Boeke, the master planner of the Sea Ranch, the pioneering ecologically sensitive development in Mendocino, two hours north of San Francisco. Boeke responded with a sweeping five-year plan for the project and then went to see if the land had the environmental quality to justify its development. The ambitious undertaking eventually had to be abandoned due to an unreliable business partner, but Turner likes to recall that during the several months the ranch was under his control, he and his partner Tom Stockton actually managed to turn it into a profitable ranching operation. Although the development project never came together, Turner valued the opportunity to work with Al Boeke, one of his chief inspirations.

STOCKTON RESIDENCE (1987)

Tom Stockton had been one of Turner's roommates at West Point, and Turner had been best man at Stockton's wedding to his high-school sweetheart, Wootsie. When the Stocktons eventually retired to Solana Beach, an oceanfront community adjoining Del Mar, he and Turner became business partners and soon made plans for a house.

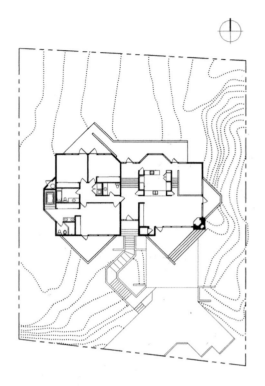

THE STOCKTON RESIDENCE WAS BUILT ON A DIFFICULT LOT WITH VAST OCEAN VIEWS, A HUGE TORREY PINE TREE AND AN ADJACENT SCENIC CANYON. THE DESIGN SOLUTION INCLUDED AN "EARTH-SHELTERED" GARAGE SET AT THE BOTTOM-MOST POINT ON THE LOT, WITH A GARDEN ON TOP, AND HALF OF THE NEXT LEVEL BUILT THREE FEET HIGHER TO AVOID DAMAGING THE MAJESTIC TREE'S ROOT SYSTEM.

The Stocktons had thoroughly inventoried the coastal region and drew up a graph based on their favorite sites in relation to their potential costs. The graph, of course, showed that the most desirable lots in the best neighborhoods cost the most. Noting that the best neighborhoods increased in value faster than the less expensive neighborhoods, Turner convinced them to follow one of his fundamental development maxims: Buy the cheapest lot in the best neighborhood, and then solve the problem that makes it the cheapest lot.

The south Del Mar site they eventually chose was challenging but admirably endowed with a view of the ocean all the way to La Jolla, and an inland

view over the Los Peñasquitos Lagoon toward San Diego to the south. Another asset was a gigantic Torrey pine tree whose branches covered half of the rear of the lot to the north. Yet another asset was an adjoining canyon to the east that harbored more large Torrey pines.

The lot's topography once more indicated the solution. Nestled in a small ravine at the lowest level of the lot, the garage was "earth-sheltered," providing a garden on top, situated just off the living room deck. The living room and the bedroom were now on the same level, but the northeast corner of the building—including the kitchen, dining room and patio—was elevated an additional three feet in order to raise the north patio high enough to avoid damaging the Torrey pines' root systems.

The house was designed in daytime and evening components, with the living, dining and kitchen areas set apart from the bedroom area. The two groupings were separated by a wide entry hall that directly framed the Torrey pine tree viewed from the north patio. To further accent the views, the roof was rotated so its hips were in the middle of the walls instead of at their corners, giving the house a sculptural feeling. Besides creating more activity in the roof design, this device emphasized the view and diagrammed the traffic patterns.

SOUTHFAIR: A LANDMARK COMMERCIAL PROJECT (1972–1981)

Southfair is an unusual mixed-use complex that successfully combines environmental sensitivity, artists' exhibition areas and, at 45,800 square feet, an exceptional setting for businesses and professional practices. Well situated within the affluent coastal community of Del Mar, this complex is just south of the Del Mar Fairgrounds with easy access to Interstate 5. Its convenient location near the freeway allows businesses to draw customers from the adjacent enclaves of La Jolla, Solana Beach and Rancho Santa Fe.

As developer, Turner's goal for the center was to create a commercial environment that would incorporate the beauty of art and nature. When completed, Southfair realized that goal with a lively mix of upscale restaurants and well-established businesses in a parklike setting graced with sculpture and fine art.

"Artistspace," an important feature of Southfair, was conceived by Turner when he was confronted with the challenge of building a 9,000-square-foot gym in the complex. After studying many gyms in the area he realized that modern gyms with their aerobic exercise classes were incompatible with an office-use mix because of the loud noise they created. To solve the problem he conceived of a solid-wall construction enclosing the gym, with another glass wall two feet from the solid wall to trap escaping sound. This glass wall would be a space for artists to show their work. It was thus called "Artistspace at Southfair." Here, contemporary works by artists, designers, architects and landscape architects are displayed on a rotating basis. Approximately five curated shows are presented each year. Exhibits have included the works of San Francisco architect Aaron Green, a collaborator of Frank Lloyd Wright, paintings by the West Coast Water-color Society, and the work of many other individuals and organizations.

The design of the center exemplifies Turner's commitment to building structures that are in harmony with the environment. From the street, Southfair gives the impression of being nestled in a park. The building nearest the boulevard is almost completely earth-sheltered, its roof and exterior wall covered with living plants. The interior, however, is bathed

THE ICONIC 45,800-SQUARE-FOOT SOUTHFAIR COMPLEX IN DEL MAR IS TURNER'S LANDMARK COMMERCIAL PROJECT. INCORPO-RATING HIS SIGNATURE DESIGN ELEMENTS AND GREEN SENSIBILITIES, THE MIXED-USE DEVELOPMENT IS A PRIME SETTING FOR BUSINESSES AND PROFESSIONAL PRACTICES.

THE "EARTH-
SHELTERED" STREET
LEVEL OF SOUTHFAIR
COMBINES SKYLIGHTS
AND DECORATIVE
LAWN SERVING BOTH
INTERIOR AND
EXTERIOR AESTHETICS,
A FORWARD-
THINKING DESIGN FOR
1972.

103

104

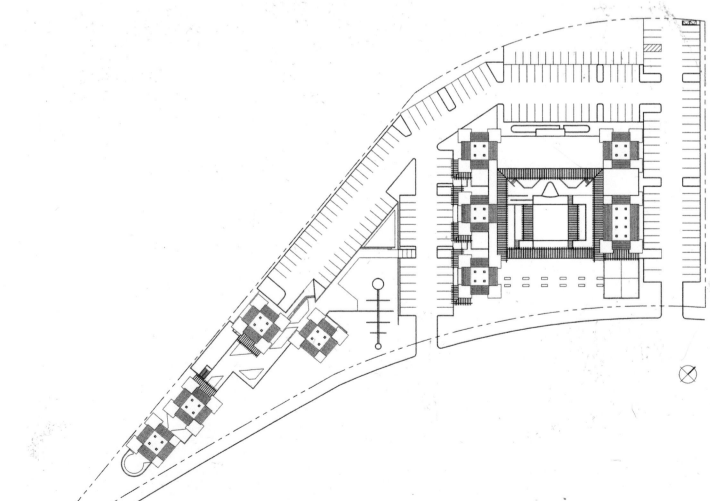

SOUTHFAIR COMBINES NATURAL ELEMENTS WITH ARTISTIC PATHWAYS, COURTYARDS AND GATHERING PLACES THAT ENHANCE COMMUNITY INTERACTION. A PERMANENT ART GALLERY, BUILT INTO THE EXTERIOR WALLS OF THE GYM, ADDS TO THE AMENITIES FOR THE MANY BUSINESSES AND PROFESSIONAL SERVICE TENANTS.

in light from skylights and from windows that face the courtyard. The low-profile redwood buildings feature private patios, trellised walkways and vented windows to take advantage of Del Mar's mild year-round climate. Each of the buildings opens to the large, center courtyard where

seating, shade, refreshments and artwork prompt employees and customers to stop and relax.

Southfair embodies a synergistic concept that successfully combines art, architecture and the natural environment. The center has not been overlooked by the public, and its unique design has received widespread publicity in both the San Diego press and architectural trade journals. It earned an award of merit in the San Diego Building Industry Association's SAM Awards competition.

THE EVOLVING TURNER RESIDENCE: 606 ZUNI DRIVE (1956–PRESENT)

Turner's first purchase in Del Mar was the lot at 606 Zuni Drive. He has continued to live in the house he built there for fifty years as his family has grown over three generations. From his study of American architecture Turner realized that he was following a path similar to our early settlers – starting out with a small house and enlarging it as the family grew in size. His expanding house plan was similar to the linear California ranch-house style; however, the Zuni house was a square of 100 feet with various setbacks, and with a cliff running through the middle of the lot. So the linear option was not available.

Turner developed a planning process that radiated from his original 600-square-foot studio-kitchen-bath above a 400-square-foot carport, all of which was pushed up against a cliff to the north and a hillside to the east. This early project had brought glimmers of the terramonic approach as he used what the land offered to full advantage, without resorting to mass grading with a bulldozer.

Over the years there have been four major additions to the basic studio. The first addition consisted of a living room, two bedrooms and a bath, all

THE ORIGINAL STUDIO,
BUILT IN 1956, WITH
KITCHEN AND BATH.

THE FINAL DESIGN OF
SECOND FLOOR WITH
CARPORT AND TWO
BEDROOMS ON THE
FIRST FLOOR.

TURNER RESIDENCE,
CURRENT SOUTH
ELEVATION AND
CARPORT.

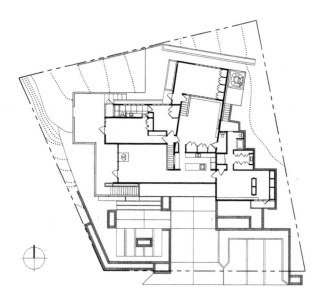

raised to the level of the studio, with decks facing west. After the original studio had been incorporated into the expanding house, a back family room was added, and a smaller studio was built to the north. The design of the house eliminates hallways to improve traffic patterns and make better use of space.

San Diego Fine Arts Festival

In 1960, Herb Turner served as Chairman of the Board of Directors of the San Diego Fine Arts Festival. The primary function of this nonprofit, educational corporation was to raise public awareness of the Realist movement by exhibiting paintings by the nation's leading Realist artists. As the sole invitation-only Realist exhibition in the country, the 20th Century American Realists Festival was enormously popular.

The first year, Turner and his fellow organizers invited only Realist artists of stature, keeping their fingers crossed that the chosen artists would accept. Fortunately, they did: Peter Hurd and John Koch, two artists of major importance, exhibited. The show, held at the San Diego Art Institute, continued successfully for several years featuring prestigious artists such as Andrew Wyeth.

Comprehensive Planning Organization, San Diego County

In the 1960s, Turner joined a subcommittee of the Environmental Quality and Natural Resources Committee of the San Diego Comprehensive Planning Organization. This organization was formed to improve the environmental quality of San Diego County, since members felt that county government was not providing adequate services in that arena. Turner thought he recognized a great opportunity to meet and learn from experts in the environmental field. He imagined that the group might host stimulating discussions about how human beings could alter their personal lives to create a better environmental future. Instead, the goal of this group was to gain control of local government planning, an effort that was thwarted by the existing political process. The result, however, was the creation of an advisory group incorporating all the cities in the county.

Del Mar Villagers

Founded in the late 1960s, Del Mar Villagers was a nonprofit organization that grew out of widespread community interest in changing the land-use rules in Del Mar by challenging the existing city zoning ordinance. Ironically, this group was originally composed of *new* residents—mostly associated with the nearby University of California campus—whose priority was city preservation. Naturally, older established residents were upset about having their city's planning process suddenly commandeered by newcomers. The disagreement divided Del Mar into two opposing camps for the next twenty years—one side for more government control and the other for individual rights.

Associated Builders and Contractors, Inc.

In 1977 Turner acted on his growing concern about the increasing influence of labor unions forcing the government to accept the much higher union wage as the "average daily wage" for government contracts. He joined the Board of Directors and the Legislative Committee of Associated Builders and Contractors, Inc. and worked with the Center for Technical Services to help develop non-union apprenticeship programs in the building industry.

Over time, Turner's dedication to the Center for Technical Services intensified, and in the 1970s he was named Chairman of the Board of Directors. In this role he worked to help the organization achieve its mission of transferring advanced technology between government services and private industry. Ideally, such technology would dramatically streamline government business affairs and bring about unprecedented efficiency. The Center's dealings with the City of San Diego were indeed successful, and produced the results for which all had hoped. However, as a result of this privately generated efficiency, the government bureaucracy felt threatened. When budgets were proposed, the bureaucracy took credit for the new-found efficiency and eliminated public funding for the Center.

The La Jolla Athenaeum

Turner had begun taking art classes at The Athenaeum in La Jolla in the late 1970s. Though he enjoyed his classes and thought highly of the institution's programs, he nevertheless saw room for improvement. The location itself was not easy to get to, the facilities were cramped, and parking was limited. Turner felt that The Athenaeum could reach a wider audience by offering satellite classes in storefront properties around the San Diego area. The school should go where the students are, he reasoned, and he submitted a formal proposal encouraging the school to do just that.

Turner's plan was to merge The Athenaeum with the New School of Architecture, which had more space than it could use. Turner himself served as the liaison between the expansion effort and the New School of Architecture. Later, The Athenaeum purchased a building near Balboa Park, south of La Jolla in San Diego, and furthered the outreach efforts that Turner had initiated.

Public Projects

In the early 1980s, Mayor Jim Tetrault formed the Village Committee, whose task was to assist development of two major commercial projects in Del Mar: The Del Mar Hotel and The Plaza at the intersection of Camino Del Mar and 15th Street.

The committee of local people familiar with development projects, including Turner, was charged with bridging the gap between the developers of these projects and the public. The public, it was felt, should be involved in their city's growth in an informal yet creative way. The committee held hearings, but with a very small public attendance. In contrast, when the formal hearings were held, the opposition showed up *en masse*, starting a battle that went on for years. Both projects were passed by the slimmest of margins.

More recently, the city of Del Mar and the public have been working together to make the Village Center more attractive and profitable.

AN ENDURING CONTRIBUTION

Through his building solutions over many years, Herb Turner has made a definitive and enduring contribution to the design of Del Mar, celebrating the region's unique rustic charm and glorious natural environment with homes and commercial buildings that reflect and build on these qualities. "My ideal design for community," Turner maintains, "combines public commonality with private individuality." His designs offer a compelling combination of contemporary lines, natural materials and colors, open space and generous light, interior-exterior interaction and lots drawn from untouched natural landscapes.

A highly visible and visited U. S. community, this village on the Pacific coast has influenced the aesthetics of many other regions with its unique planning solutions and architectural style, which can be traced to a few local visionaries, Herbert Turner among them.

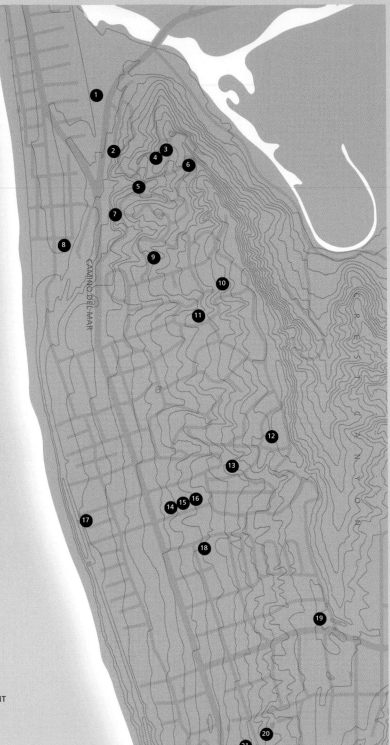

114

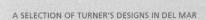

A SELECTION OF TURNER'S DESIGNS IN DEL MAR

1. SOUTHFAIR
2. DURANTE HOUSE
3. LIGHTHALL HOUSE
4. HOFHEIMER HOUSE
5. BERKICH HOUSE
6. TRONESON HOUSE
7. MCCAMEY HOUSE
8. COAST DEL MAR
9. RYPINSKI HOUSE
10. TURNER HOUSE
11. CATES HOUSE
12. SOUTHWORTH HOUSE
13. COWETT HOUSE
14, 15, 16. NINTH STREET DEVELOPMENT
17. WALBURGER APPARTMENTS
18. PARK PLACE CONDOMINIUMS
19. UPDIKE HOUSE
20. RICHARDSON HOUSE
21. SINNOTT HOUSE
22. HELLEN HOUSE
23. REESE HOUSE
24. STOCKTON HOUSE
25. DAVIS HOUSE

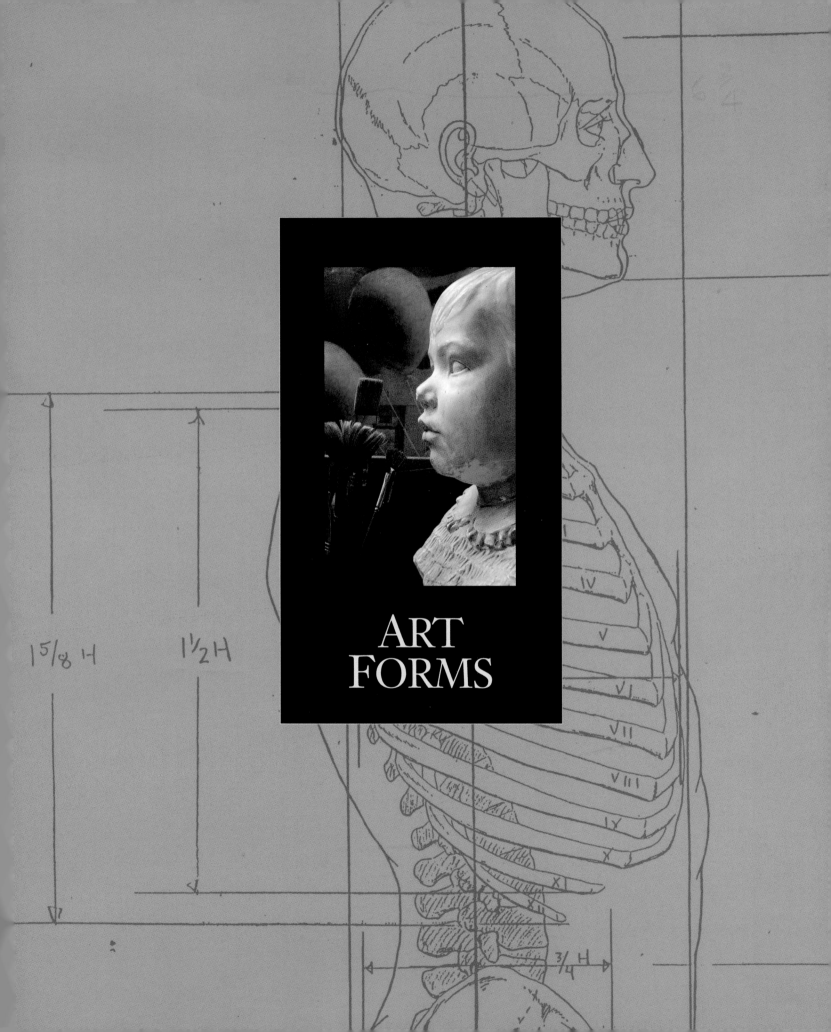

ART
FORMS

Three art forms—painting, architecture and sculpture—each informing the others, through the mind and heart and hands of Herbert Turner.

A Path to Self-Discovery

Turner's unique odyssey has combined seemingly contradictory personality traits, instincts, processes and objectives that have time and again spawned novel approaches and solutions, and in sum have brought about a body of work that has inspired countless lives, and made significant contributions to twentieth-century architecture and painting.

In his early twenties, Turner had been surprised as his inner artist emerged in the context of a difficult two years of preparation for entrance into the West Point military academy. After all, he was an athlete, and on his way to becoming an officer in the army. Yet he delighted in the subtle power of painted gestures, and found himself one of the few men in a group of mostly women behind the easels in the art class he took during summer break. By his second year at West Point, having achieved through fierce determination and discipline his initial goal of admission into the world's most prestigious military academy, he had again allowed his artistic side an opening. Collecting reference books from the academy library and art tools from the Graphics department, he began to draw again. He found other cadets interested in art as well, and a few mentors, who praised his talents and offered guidance and support.

Turner still had an underlying unease with the juxtaposition of his realities, asking himself, "How can I be at West Point, doing art?" An examination of his mental fitness proved he was psychologically sound, and an analysis of his aptitudes indicated he had the right stuff for a military officer. To his surprise, the tests also showed he was equally well-suited to be an artist or an architect. Reassured, he went ahead and followed his instincts and did what only Herb Turner would do: He formed West Point's first art club.

After a soccer injury in his final year at West Point derailed his military career, he realized that art was necessarily becoming for him more than a hobby. His creative education accelerated, with the instruction of Naum Los and Robert Brackman, an increasing attraction to egg tempera painting, and a growing affinity for the works of American Regionalist masters Andrew Wyeth and Edward Hopper. He was beginning to formulate in his paintings a response to the modern human condition and context. And he was cultivating another artistic passion, sculpture, with the profound genius of Auguste Rodin as his inspiration and influence.

While his artist persona was forming, Turner's strategic approach to his life course kept bringing him back to architecture. Understanding that painting and sculpture were unlikely to provide more than a and responding to his family heritage as a builder (his father and grandfather were both builders), he began to explore his potential in the world of architecture. Inspired by architecture's modern masters, and honing his career strategy, he sought out and obtained an apprenticeship with John Lloyd Wright in Del Mar. His path as an architect-builder unfolded from there, but with it the two other disciplines of painting and sculpture would be followed in parallel, during his entire life.

Synergy and the Creative Process

Principles and techniques passed on from his teachers and the work of the masters combine with his personal artistic sensibilities in Turner's creative process, whether he's working on a painting, a sculpture or an architectural project. Turner's work, as a whole, evidences the benefit he has realized from the synergies inherent in his three artistic pursuits. While he approaches his life and acts of creation with the values of a committed artist, his career path has leveraged his outward talents as a leader, translating his military ambitions into the front lines of business, *building* buildings as well as designing them.

The common thread in Turner's art forms is *depth*: an understanding and use of depth in all its meanings. Rodin's example taught him to "think in depth." The thumb pushes *into* the clay, shaping space; the pencil defines walls and floors, carving out a living space.

In Turner's words, "A building has two kinds of depth, interior and exterior, and they are inextricably linked." The building is placed against the hillside, and to fit in with the trees and boulders and bring about just the right views with just the right amount of open space, rooms are pushed out, ceilings raised, windows stretched, beams elongated. The view out a

CRUCIFIXION
1966
EGG TEMPERA AND
CASEIN ON MASONITE
(DETAIL)

119

window—which in Turner's designs is *never* small and often wall-sized—is part of the depth of the room. Solidity and transparency, built structure and existing landscape, form and flow, the skeleton and the flesh, are all carefully balanced in an organic whole.

Turner's work is indeed organic, with a profound respect for both the natural environment and the complex patterns of life. On the following pages are "galleries" of Turner's paintings, buildings and sculptures. His painting is a means to study the human condition and convey his personal responses to the modern world. His architecture is a living art form, weaving together the aesthetic and functional solutions that enhance and harmonize the human landscape. Finally, sculpture is his direct, tactile experience of the human form and the living world to which it belongs.

"Turner's realistic, representational canvases possess a "slice of life" candidness

PAINTINGS

as if frozen in time by the camera's eye. Yet there is an irony and a sense of activism that subtly directs the action of the paintings to important concerns of the artist: the environment, the family and the human rights issues of personal freedom and quality of life. These issues are also important in the houses and communities that Turner designs, where the preservation of the environment and how a family or individual exists within the community are of vital concern. It is in his paintings, however, that he has the opportunity to address these issues directly, manipulating his subjects to create a more overt narrative."

— Jim Reed, Curator, Riverside Art Museum

The Regionalist

Inspired by artists he loved, whose works depicted classic architectural designs and landscapes, and by the scenic wonder of his home in Saranac Lake in upstate New York, and propelled by his artistic education, Turner came to the American Regionalist tradition, with a specific interest in the work of Edward Hopper and Andrew Wyeth. It was Wyeth who led Turner to experiment with the relatively obscure medium of egg tempera. Although he has worked in acrylic and oil, as well as ink and watercolor, the alchemical quality of egg tempera attracted his loyalty early, and it has been his primary medium of expression in paint.

For Turner, painting has always been a very personal endeavor, and while his work has been shown at many gallery exhibits across the United States, he has avoided the world of art commerce, rarely selling his canvases. His work is recognized as belonging to the American Regionalism movement that began in the 1930s, with the Midwestern artists Thomas Hart Benton, Grant Wood and John Steuart Curry, though the related Social Realism school also influenced Turner's chosen style and purpose.

The paintings in this gallery section are captioned by the artist himself, or, as noted, by Jim Reed, curator of the Riverside Art Museum.

EGG TEMPERA

Egg tempera is a painting technique that was popular in southern Europe in the Middle Ages, in which egg yolk is mixed with a paste of pigment and water, the egg serving as the binder. Egg tempera painting is often done on a wood or Masonite panel covered with gesso, a thin, white plasterlike coating. Paint is usually applied with fine, pointed brushes, so shapes and details can be exact and strong. The artist may add water to thin the paint and keep it flowing, but egg tempera generally dries very quickly. When dry, the paint is water-resistant, so new brush strokes don't blend easily with older strokes. Tones are built up by layering fine strokes over one another. Varnish is often applied to protect the surface from scratching, and colors stand up well over time.

GEORGIE JOE CHINESE
VILLAGE
1956
OIL ON CANVAS
28 X 44 INCHES

One reason I painted
this piece was to
memorialize the
pleasant times that
John Lloyd Wright, his
wife Frances and I had
at Georgie Joe's
restaurant while I was
an apprentice to Mr.
Wright. Furthermore,
this Edward Hopper–
like scene, including
both Georgie Joe and
a watercolor of the Del
Mar fairgrounds by
Dong Kingman, was a
direct response to my
teacher Robert
Brackman's instruction
to remove traces of his
style.

BLACK JUG AND
DEGAS PRINT
1957
OIL ON CANVAS
23 X 15 INCHES

This was the first still
life I painted in my Del
Mar studio, which was
still under construction
at the time. Whereas
most paintings of this
kind are horizontal, I
felt a vertical thrust
for this piece would be
more effective. The
subject matter was all
locally obtained, for
me a welcome to
California. It ended up
being the first painting
I exhibited, and it won
First Place in the
Carlsbad-Oceanside
annual exhibit of local
artists.

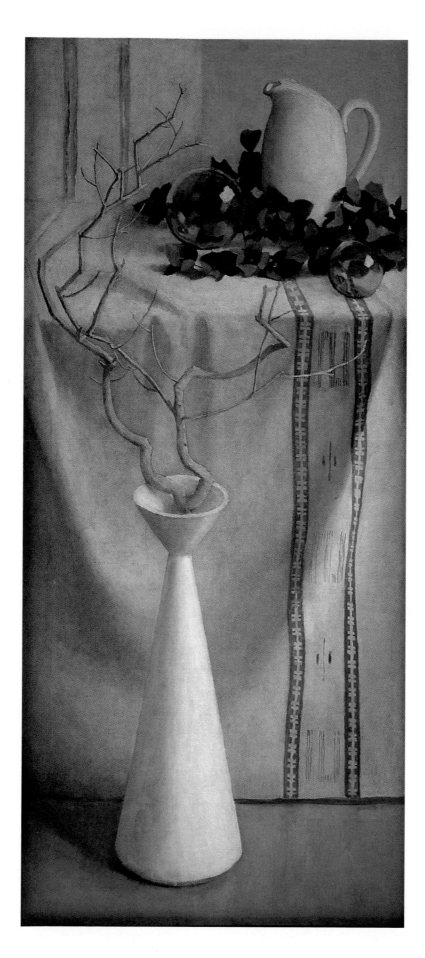

CALIFORNIA STILL LIFE
1958
OIL ON CANVAS
40 X 18 INCHES

Another vertical still
life composition
featuring local
elements—the blanket
from Tijuana, the vase
from Laguna Beach,
the dried plant from
the Anza-Borrego
Desert, and a red
bougainvillea from
Del Mar. The colors of
red, white and blue
symbolized an
American take on
local color.

PINK PETTICOAT
1958
OIL ON CANVAS
20 X 40 INCHES

My wife's petticoat inspired this piece, decidedly
horizontal. The violin and the implied ballet
dancer brought to mind the work of Degas,
hence the incorporated prints by Degas and his
friend Manet. This piece is more reflective of my
East Coast sensibilities.

CUDAHY
1963
OIL ON CANVAS
36 X 20 INCHES

"In the foreground of
the painting, we
witness nature
abused. What could
have been natural
wetlands and a refuge
for wildlife has been
subjugated by the
distant meat
processing plant, its
red, white and blue
reflection in the
murky waters making
a dim commentary on
the American dream."
—Jim Reed, Curator,
Riverside Art Museum

GLIDING GULL
1961
OIL ON CANVAS
32 X 45 INCHES

This painting emerged from my desire to work outside the studio, and explore the beauty of La Jolla Cove, just south of Del Mar. The gull flying into my view inspired this composition, contrasting the energetic movement of the gull with the "static movement" of the rock forms. This was a successful experiment in achieving three-dimensionality on a two-cimensional surface, working with the light, the water and the space enclosed by the cliff.

129

LA JOLLA COVE
1964
OIL ON CANVAS
24 X 40 INCHES

Painted over three
years, this was meant
to be a scenic painting,
period. La Jolla Cove
offers a unique and
dramatic natural
beauty that is a
favorite subject for
amateur and
professional
photographers.
I wanted to capture
this natural wonder in
oil for its sheer beauty
– and to create an
appealing piece of art
on a par with those
I saw in local galleries.
But I never did actually
try to sell it.

HIDDEN COVE
1962
OIL ON CANVAS
20 X 40 INCHES

I was taken by the interplay of sunlight and water on the cliffs and the triangular geometry converging on the sandy beach. The use of earthen tones for the environment sets off the energy of the colorful swimmers at the convergence of multiple triangles.

132

133

DEATH OF A SPARROW
1964
CASEIN AND OIL ON MASONITE
36 X 48 INCHES

"*Death of a Sparrow* is ripe with symbols and contradictions. Here we witness life and death, flight and stillness, hunter and prey. The foreground-background contrast presents a life-and-death comparison between the barren ground and lush vegetation; the circle of life goes on."
—*Jim Reed, Curator, Riverside Art Museum*

134

CRUCIFIXION
1966
EGG TEMPERA AND CASEIN ON
MASONITE
20 X 28 INCHES

This was an early experiment
combining egg tempera with casein
painting (a milk-based technique
used in Egyptian temples, the oldest
organic painting medium). The
casein was used on the cross, which
brought it forward from the
background scene, painted with the
egg tempera.

"*Crucifixion* gives a direct, if
symbolic, warning to the future of
the environment. In a convention
reminiscent of a canvas of Georgia
O'Keeffe, Turner allows a cross to
partition the canvas into four
segments. We see this pastoral
setting divided and fragmented, the
graveyard a thing of the past and if
we are not careful, this entire scene
will be as well. Concerns of family,
relationships and speed of life are
all apparent in this work."
—*Jim Reed, Curator,*
Riverside Art Museum

GENERATIONS
1968
OIL AND MAROGER ON MASONITE
23 X 37 INCHES

One day I was talking to my grand-
mother-in-law, Dandy, when the child
next door burst out of the house,
slammed the door and created a loud
noise. Dandy's quiet environment was
lost. My immediate feeling was of
annoyance with the child who had made
the disturbance, but I realized in this
moment that this was simply an
intersection of very different realities. I
saw Dandy in her restricted and quiet
environment, in sharp contrast to the
lively world of the child. It was the
contrast of ages and stages and their
differing modes of time that inspired this
painting.

FREEDOM AND CONFINEMENT

1968

TEMPERA AND ACRYLIC ON MASONITE

36 X 48 INCHES

The motorcycle is the symbol of freedom, a means of transportation and a state of mind for many people. If one chooses, it can become a lifestyle that will control the manner of dress, language, attitude, beliefs and points of view. The statue is a symbol of religion with a promise of freedom. Once adopted, the world of religion will expect us to conform to a lifestyle, manner of dress, language, attitude, beliefs and point of view in line with its teachings. Which freedom is less confining? The freedom to move physically from place to place confined to a motorcycle, or the freedom of meditation, which confines us to a place but allows us to transcend the trivia of our everyday life? The viewer must choose to maintain his freedom within the form of confinement that he selects.

THE MEMORIAL PARK
AND THE CEMETERY
1969
EGG TEMPERA ON
MASONITE
24 X 63 INCHES

After I had been in California for a while and had attended a few funeral services, I went back to Saranac Lake, a small town in upstate New York, for my father's funeral. The contrast in the rituals of eastern services with those in California was magnified by this experience. In small eastern towns every passing is a personal grief for that individual community. Time is set aside for mourning. Friends and relatives you haven't seen in years mourn with the family; it is a tremendously emotional experience. In California one is not buried in a cemetery but rather ensconced in a memorial park owned and managed by an impersonal corporation. I have also found myself trapped in the impersonal culture that spawns this practice, when I have been too busy to attend a friend's memorial service. This two-panel painting is a protest painting, not so much against the commercialism of passing in California, but against the impersonal treatment of it.

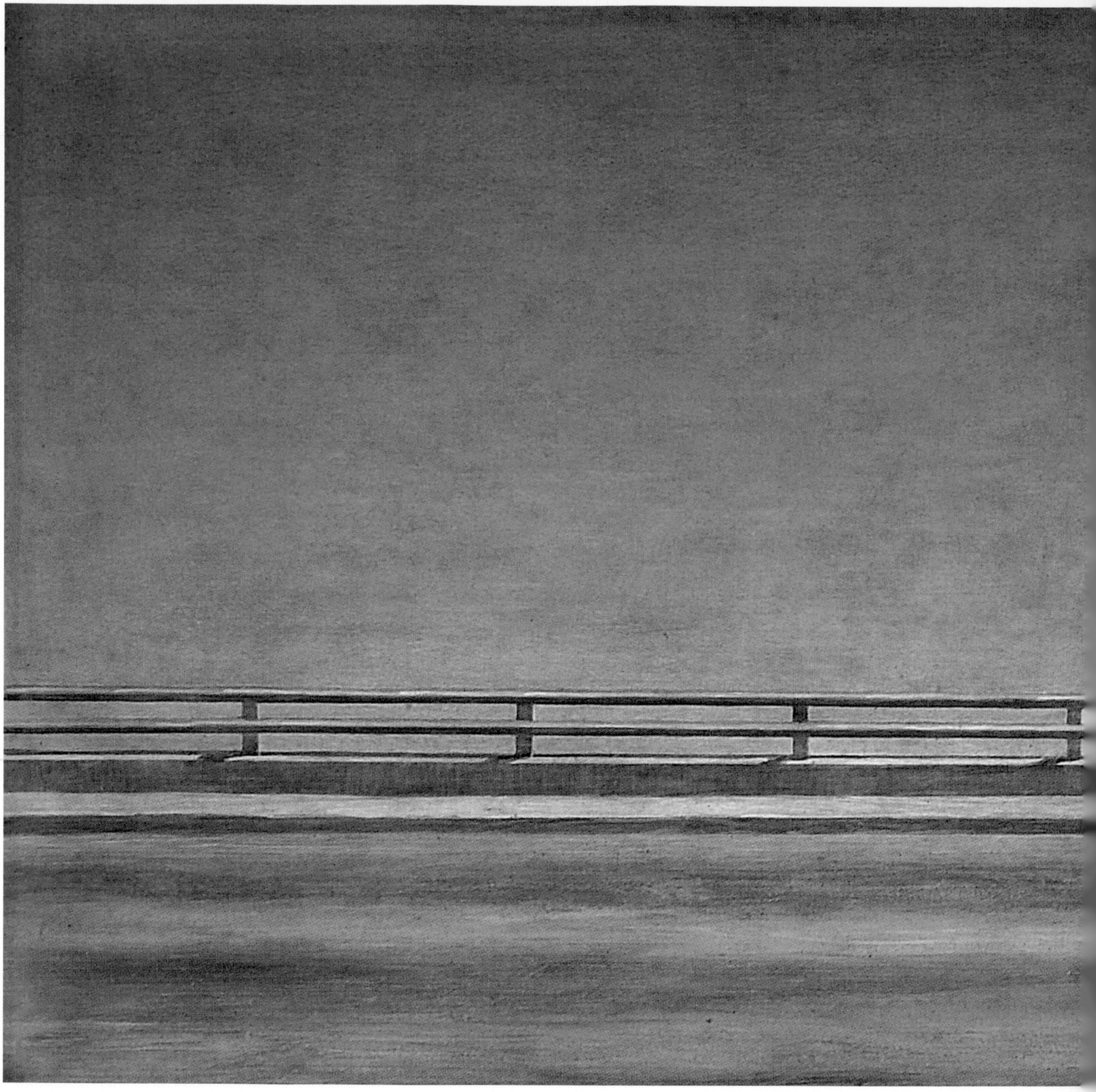

FUTURE SHOCK

1970

EGG TEMPERA ON

MASONITE

14 X 22 INCHES

"Future Shock exhibits the ability of the past to adapt to the present. In true Hopperesque fashion, Turner renders a solo Victorian structure, the last vestiges of a gentler, slower age, cut off by an expressway. Although the structure has adapted to the current age, nostalgia for a piece of the past is evident.""

—*Jim Reed, Curator,*

Riverside Art Museum

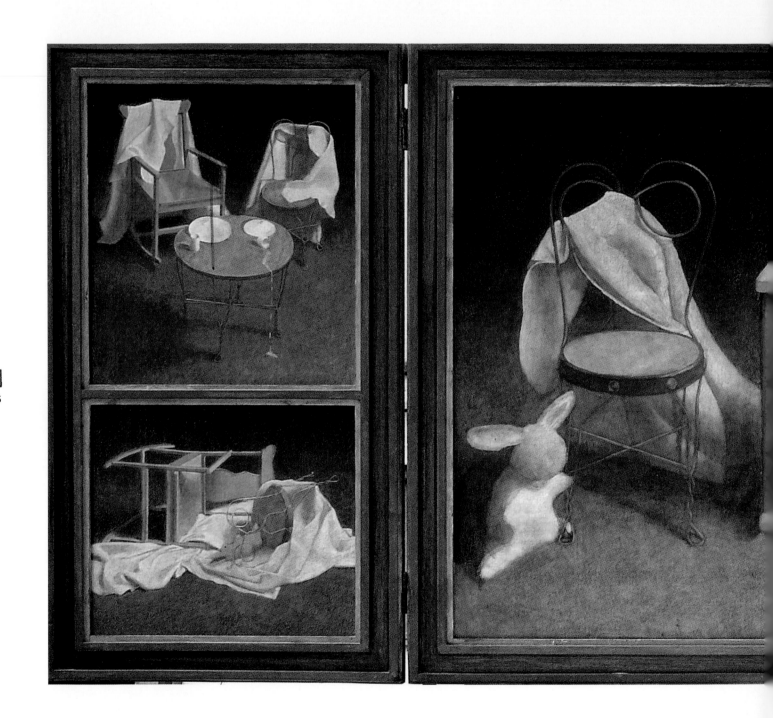

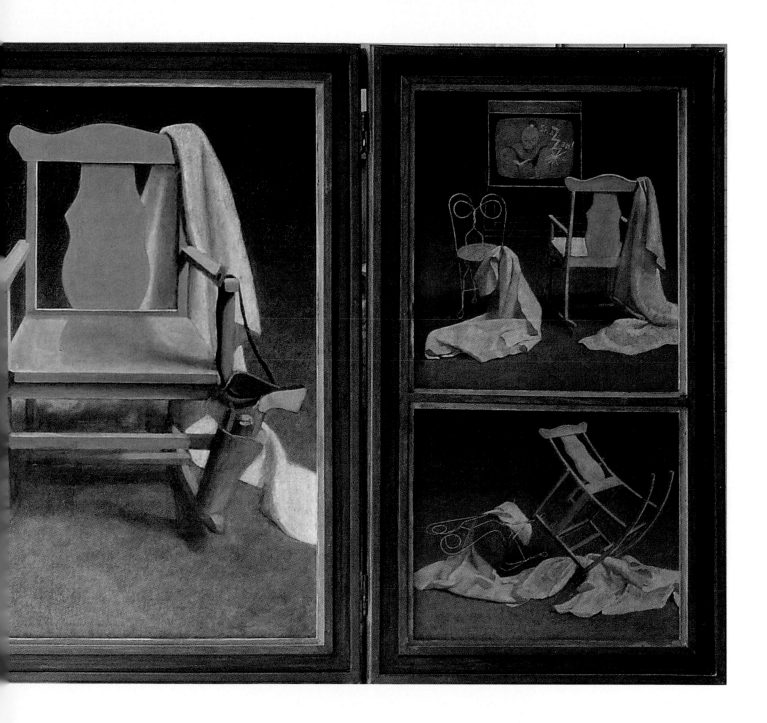

BRENT AND RACHEL
1976
CASEIN AND OIL ON
MASONITE
24 X 60 INCHES

Before we had our two children, my wife and I agreed that we wouldn't bore everyone with cute studio portraits of them. Wrong. We did. Worse, we put together entire albums. This painting is meant to be an album, a formal portrait, but conveying snapshots of the children's daily life.

MAKE LOVE, NOT WAR
1974
EGG TEMPERA ON MASONITE
31 X 44 INCHES

"*Make Love Not War* . . . deals with the
conflict of the Vietnam War and the shifting
of political and ethical positions between
the generations. Two cars pass each other.
The reflection of a passing truck is seen in
the windows of the more prominent VW
bus. Each driver observes the other at a
distance, neither interested in sharing views
as they speed relentlessly on in the direction
of their political alliances."
—*Jim Reed, Curator,*
Riverside Art Museum

148

FIRST DAY SCHOOL BUS
EGG TEMPERA ON PANEL
18 X 24 INCHES

150

My son Brent. His face said it all.

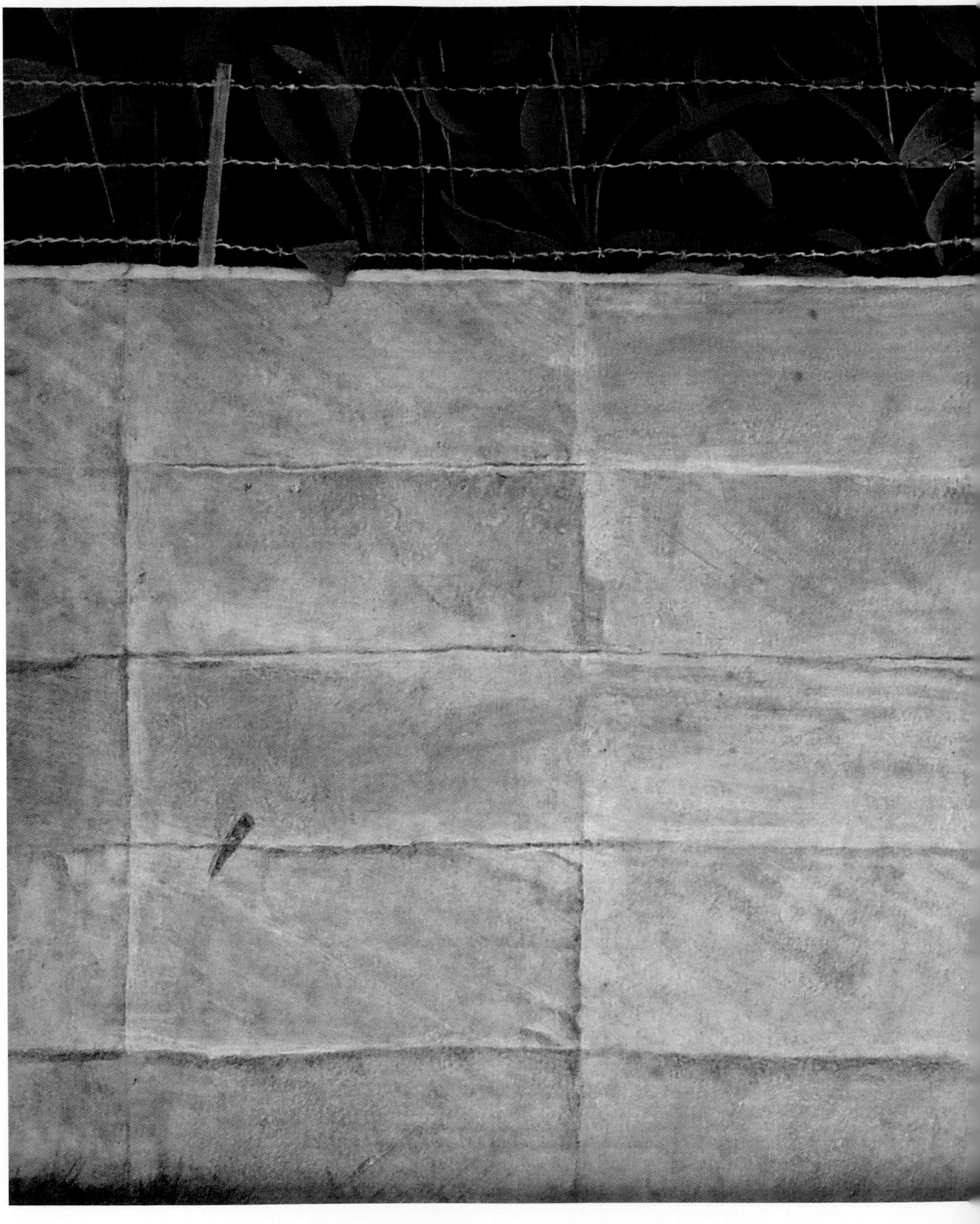

WALLING IN,
WALLING OUT
1980
EGG TEMPERA AND
CASEIN ON MASONITE
16 X 24 INCHES

This painting is a
contemporary visual
interpretation of poet
Robert Frost's
question, "Who are we
walling in and who are
we walling out?" The
inspiration for this
painting came from a
conflict in the Del Mar
community between
the established
residents and students
from the nearby
University of
California, when this
very question arose in
a discussion with
friends.

153

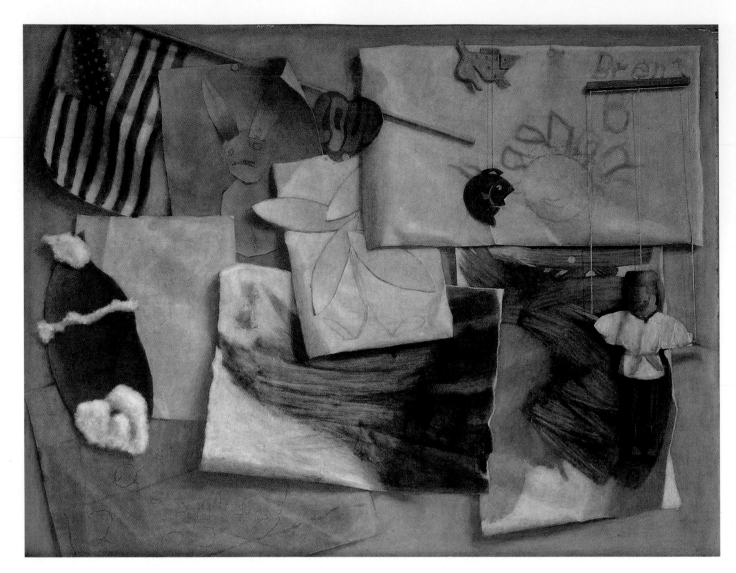

BRENT'S WALL
1970
EGG TEMPERA ON MASONITE
24 X 32 INCHES

This is a pictorial expression of
the innocence of the child as
opposed to the harsh realities of
the adult world in time of war.
Puppet government, flower
children, population explosion,
welfare state, the blood of war
across the ocean.

The *trompe l'oeil* ("fool-the-
eye") technique used here
originated in the mid-eighteenth
century and is seldom attempted
in egg tempera.

THE GREAT AMERICAN
BATHROOM AND RUBBER DUCK
1977
EGG TEMPERA ON MASONITE
22 X 36 INCHES

In California the bathroom has
become a status symbol, and
therefore has often required
much of my attention in the
homes I have built. What for me,
in my small-town East Coast
upbringing, was a humble,
functional facility, is now a high
altar of social ranking. The rubber
duck adds a touch of everyday
playfulness to the contrived
elegance.

GENE'S BLUE DODGE
1991
OIL ON MASONITE
20 X 32 INCHES

One of the great freedoms that this country offers is the electoral process. However this freedom has a price. Partisan politics, hostility, belief systems and Being Right all seem to pollute the process. During this particular election, my friend Gene Schwartz and I were supporting Pete Wilson, a Republican, and our friend Dick Roe, a Democrat. Someone smashed the window of Gene's car. We didn't know if it was a malcontent Republican or a malcontent Democrat.

157

Gene wrote this in an article in the *Del Mar Surfcomber:* "The shattered glass of my already failing Dodge's window reminds me that we can only keep trying to perfect ourselves and the world around us. I will continue to have highly partisan views about things. I think I will probably continue trying to be a bridge-builder between people I value, but mainly I am into win/win. And though the random rocks may fly I will not cast any stones where I can help myself not to. And when I do, I know I will pay the price and that is the way it is."

After reading this article I was motivated to produce this painting as a protest against violence and also as a tribute to my friend Gene Schwartz.

NEW WARRIOR

1998

EGG TEMPERA ON

MASONITE

24 X 46 INCHES

A child playing soldier in a World War II relic. For me this was a potent symbol of past wars and, unfortunately, future wars. The massiveness of the machine seems to threaten the vulnerable child.

(PAGES 160–161)
LOSANGELIZATION
1995
CASEIN AND OIL ON
MASONITE
38 X 70 INCHES

"In *Losangelization*
our view of the
encroaching
suburbanization is
impaired by a large
earth mover clearing
the rubble of Nature.
In its wake, a mindless
grid community of
identical houses
springs forth,
obliterating Nature
rather than
communing with it."
—*Jim Reed, Curator,
Riverside Art Museum*

162

This painting is my
statement on the
thoughtless
destruction of our
natural environment
by developers who
build tract homes by
the millions. As an
architect-builder, I
used to build houses
for $11 a square foot
as compared to today's
$250 to $300 a foot.
With the relentless
inflation of real estate
costs, tract housing
has brought a higher
standard of living to
millions. The paradox
is that we are left with
a destroyed natural
landscape and
profound design
mediocrity.

THE GREAT AMERICAN
PARADE
1987
24 X 123 INCHES, IN
THREE PANELS

*The Great American
Parade* is a parade of
life, time and symbols.
The buildings
symbolize spectators
viewing the parade,
the balloons symbolize
people marching, the
air trails in the sky
symbolize military
presence, and of
course the flag
symbolizes the
government. However,
the major symbolism
concerns the passage
of time, from unity in
the Depression of the
1930s and WWII, to
California in the 1950s
and 60s, to the
fractured condition of
more recent times.

ARCHITECTURE

"Herbert Turner is an artist, not only with the brush but in his building designs and his ability to bring them into expression, for he can adjust himself to the movement of life. He feels that architecture must be elevating in its way as the trees and flowers are in their way, for only so can architecture be worthy of its high rank as fine art."

—*Frances Wright*

Architect and Builder

As a master builder-architect, Herb Turner has made vital contributions to the cultural and aesthetic character of the city of Del Mar and the surrounding Southern California region. On the vanguard of modern regional architecture as well as the green design movement, Turner has maintained a creative vision that originated in the organic approach of Louis Sullivan and Frank Lloyd Wright, and is expressed in his own terramonic approach to design (described on page 95). Arising out of a sound business foundation and a builder's skills and resources, each of his projects shows an integrity fostered by the control he maintains over the building process from conception to completion.

Turner has always approached his architectural design work as he has approached his painting and sculpture—as an artist on the path of discovery. Because of this view, he has always found it difficult to quantify this design work in monetary terms. But he has balanced the equation of his livelihood through the profitable business of building. The result is that each of his building projects embodies a holistic creative process that continues long after the initial financial transactions and construction. Turner's buildings, like this paintings, cannot be valued solely in dollars. They must be appraised for what they are: modern classics. As Louis Sullivan observed, "The objective value of a building may be the dollar value when the construction is done. But sooner or later it is the subjective value that becomes money value, and the lack of subjective value, sooner or later, money loss."

Taking Le Corbusier's maxim "a house is a machine for living in" into account, along with the Sullivan's organic forms and Wright's geometric extrapolations of nature's primary patterns, Turner arrived at his own distinctive style and creative methodology as a builder-architect. To him the process is not as simple as combining architecture and landscaping—that is, designing a building and an exterior environment for it. Rather, he views "architecture plus landscape, as one thing." Similarly, for Turner a finished building is not just about the functionality of physical events within it, but also very much about the interior, psychological experience of the *people* living there. He views the experience of living and the environment for living as one integrated whole.

People who love their homes, and groups who love their buildings, preserve them. This is the ultimate sustainability in Turner's view. Likewise, restoration can be a sustainable and thus ultimately a green solution. *Life* is the point, and for Turner life is an integrated process in which architecture is a profoundly important part of human experience, even if its importance often goes unrecognized. Often identified as an early green architect, Turner agrees that environmental sensitivity is an essential ingredient for success, but he sees his work as "not so much about life being sustained, as it is about life *thriving*."

TURNER'S DRAFTING
TABLE

RYPINSKI RESIDENCE

This house, designed for a vice president of the Sierra Club, was built on two narrow lots. I positioned the house up on the northern edge of the property to allow the maximum exterior expanse. The trees and plants on the slope were all left as they were. We had also considered a two-story house, but I felt it was far too overpowering for the beautiful setting, and the client agreed once I showed him a finished design. The studio roofline with 14-foot windows gives visual access to the magnificent trees, the wall of the canyon and the sky. Cars were kept on the lower level out of view. The expansive view allows the residents to "visually live in the open space."

PARK PLACE RESIDENCES

The Park Place development includes ten individual lots that were originally zoned in 1880. The property has a cliff running through its entire length, which I wanted to preserve completely, so I positioned the houses either above or below it, and did no grading at all. I left the space open and natural, fitting the houses in carefully for views and the shared "park" setting. They were built and sold one at a time over three years. Park Place has endured as a unique community in a fabulous setting. The people all seem very happy there.

HELLEN RESIDENCE

The clients had a set of plans for a house from a well-known architect. They asked me to find an ocean-view lot in Del Mar, which I did—one of the last available. A long flat lot with a cliff, it required a strategic design to take advantage of the view, with the second-story living room jutting out over the cliff. The client was skeptical of the design changes at first, but was thoroughly convinced once he saw the view for himself as the house was framed.

COWETT RESIDENCE

The Cowett residence was envisioned as a "house in the trees," very much
about building with nature and living in nature. The two-story structure has
the living room and master bedrooms up on top, and children's quarters
downstairs. The oriental design touches—bridges and courtyard—help to keep
the living spaces private. This is one of my favorite examples of terramonic
design.

STOCKTON RESIDENCE

This property features a stunning Torrey pine tree at the top of the lot, and a setting that affords a spectacular panoramic view of the Pacific, and the village of La Jolla to the south. The garage is on the lower level, with an earth-shelter roof. The house has five decks, and the interior experience of the sky and trees is dramatic, thanks to the position of the house, the windows and the vaulted ceiling, which draws the exterior space into the middle of the house.

SCULPTURE

For Herb Turner, sculpture has been an important art form, not only for the sculpture itself but for the way it has influenced the quality of his painting as he learned to "think in depth" and to understand texture and light. Sculpture also influenced his architectural approach, pushing it toward more organic sensibilities: He sees a building as a skeleton initially, designing its form and adding the organs, muscles and skin until it comes fully alive. But above all, sculpture is for Turner his most personal art form. It remains an ongoing process of discovery and discipline.

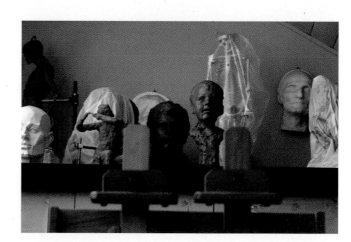

SCULPTURES IN PROGRESS IN THE ARTIST'S STUDIO.

A Life Student of Rodin

Turner began working in sculpture under Naum Los (see page 38) at the same time he began painting in earnest. Los introduced him to the work of Auguste Rodin, who may have been the most powerful single influence on Turner as an artist. Taken by the passion and depth of Rodin's work, Turner sought to fully understand and learn from this modern master. In so doing he came across Rodin's "Testament," which he laboriously translated from the French himself (see page 42), so as to fully appreciate and transmit this passionate "call to the artist."

JOAN

MID-1950s

YOUNG GIRL

MID-1950s

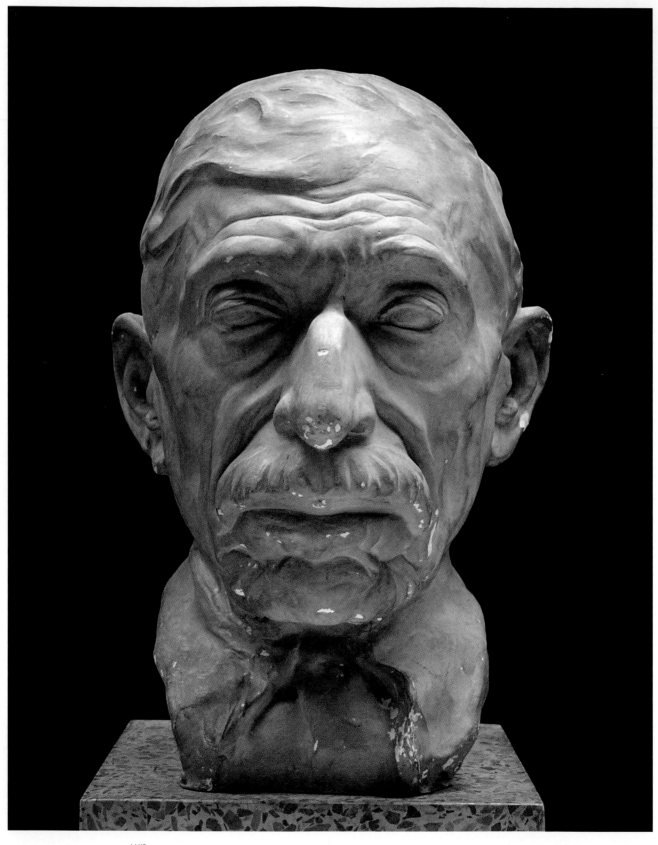

LUIS

MID-1950s

Toward
A Greener
Future

Emergence of a Green Architect

People develop a "sense of place" through experience and knowledge of a particular area. . . . The feel of the sun on your face or the rain on your back, the rough and smooth textures of the land, the color of the sky at morning and sunset . . . are environmental influences that help to define a place. Memories of personal and cultural experiences over time make a place special . . . Developing a sense of place helps people identify with their region and with each other. A strong sense of place can lead to more sensitive stewardship of our . . . natural environment.

—Tom Wood, makingsenseofplace.com

SARANAC LAKE, NEW YORK, IN WINTER.

Herb Turner's love for nature stems from his earliest days. As a boy growing up in the varied and beautiful Adirondacks region, he was an active member of the Boy Scouts. As an Eagle Scout, he spent most of his summers in the woods and on the water, serving as a camp counselor. Typical of his summer experiences, at the end of the camp session one year, he and other counselors took a 300-mile canoe trip. His immersion in the natural world inspired an increasing appreciation for organic forms and systems, as his instincts for design and building began to surface in his teenage years.

Turner's desire to create habitable spaces in harmony with and in the midst of nature began to take shape in his adolescence. As teenagers, Turner and his friends would go ice fishing in the winter using a crudely constructed shanty as a transportable shelter that could be dragged onto the ice and strategically positioned. Built from a wood frame attached to timber runners, covered with salvaged cardboard and a waterproof roof, and outfitted with a wood-burning stove and other comforts, the shanty had a wood floor with two holes to fish through. Each winter, they dragged it to neighboring Lower Saranac Lake and positioned it over holes they had dug in the ice.

Also influential during his adolescent years were his mother's stories about his grandfather, Augustine Branch, a founding partner of Branch and Callaghan, one of the largest construction firms in the Adirondacks region. Turner's dogged determination to overcome whatever obstacles were in his way was undoubtedly inherited from his grandfather, either directly through the genes or through the rich legacy of the stories his mother told him.

Before Augustine Branch settled at Saranac Lake, he built a hotel between two lakes in a high mountain pass called the Cascades. Turner was fascinated to hear of his grandfather surmounting obstacles to complete the challenging project—building the shell in the summer and finishing the interiors during the winter, if and when he could gain access to the site through the often-closed mountain roads.

One of the most dramatic stories his mother told him was about the tragic fire that destroyed the original Branch and Callaghan lumber mill and yard. Turner's grandparents were coming back from Lake Placid in their horse-drawn buggy. About ten miles from Saranac Lake, they were stunned to see a large cloud of smoke billowing over the water. His grandfather knew it had to be the mill on fire, as there was nothing else large enough to produce that much smoke. Whipping his horse into a near gallop, he arrived at the mill to find complete devastation. But in the coming months, he rebuilt the mill complex, much larger than before.

Augustine Branch had had only a sixth-grade education, but he developed formidable skills as a craftsman. One of his favorite pieces was a roll-top bird's-eye maple and cherry desk he built for himself. When Turner moved to California, the desk was shipped to him in Del Mar, where it remains as a fond reminder of his family heritage.

THE BRANCH AND CALLAGHAN LUMBER MILL COMPLEX WAS DESTROYED BY FIRE.

TURNER'S GRAND-
FATHER, AUGUSTINE
BRANCH, REBUILT THE
BRANCH AND
CALLAGHAN MILL
COMPLEX AFTER THE
FIRE.

TURNER'S EXPERIENCE
OUTDOORS IN THE
ADIRONDACKS WAS A
FOUNDATION FOR HIS
UNDERSTANDING OF
THE IMPORTANCE OF A
SENSE OF PLACE AND
FOR HIS REGIONALIST
APPROACH TO
ARCHITECTURE.

Though he didn't realize it until much later, another major influence in the development of Turner's architecture was his familiarity with the majestic Adirondacks camps that had been built at the beginning of the twentieth century. These wildly romantic lodges, built by local guides, carpenters and craftsmen, directly influenced his later choice of an idiosyncratic regional style. Turner realized that the Adirondacks was a unique place with unique characteristics in both its natural and built environments. "When you passed through Lake George, going south, you were clearly out of the region," Turner recalls, "and coming back in through Lake George, you instantly knew you were close to home. As a teenager, I remember the pronounced feeling of *home* that I felt then, and can still feel today."

As an art student in New York City, exposed to the work of Frank Lloyd Wright and the Prairie School, Turner immediately recognized similarities between Wright's work and the regional expression of the Adirondacks style. Meanwhile, regionalism emerged as a movement in American art, and as painters like Thomas Hart Benton, Grant Wood and John Steuart Curry appeared on the scene, Turner grew to view America in its width and breadth as an assembly of artistic and architectural regions, each with its own particular identity.

Across the country, successive waves of immigrants had placed their stamp on the natural environment in ways that often retained the hallmarks of their own visual history. In attempting to re-create the settlements of their past, the new arrivals had evolved a distinct regional expression that alluded to historical models but were nevertheless uniquely suited to their present surroundings. Turner realized that the artistic and architectural value of these various regions had not earned the recognition it deserved.

In 1951, after completing his New York schooling, Turner took a road trip to visit his friend Steve White, and also to investigate Frank Lloyd Wright's Taliesin compound near Spring Green, Wisconsin. He stopped en route to visit the fabled Cranbrook Academy of Art, located in southwest Michigan near the community of Bloomfield Hills, where at one time his mentor Mr. Naum Los had been a visiting instructor. Founded in the early 1900s and famous for architect Eliel Saarinen's strikingly well-integrated overall design, Cranbrook was unlike anything that existed elsewhere in America at the time. Saarinen's landmark buildings, carefully sited on grounds that included extensive formal gardens replete with outdoor sculptures and set amid natural woods, lakes, and waterways, made a marked impression on Turner, who began to see the possibilities inherent in Cranbrook's fusion of architecture, sculpture and crafts integrated into the environment.

The tranquility of Cranbrook, in an environment that was not just orderly, clean and peaceful but all-encompassing, was not lost on Turner. Proceeding on his way to Taliesin, he anticipated experiencing a much different vision. Wright's architectural expression, he felt, was more rugged, born from the land, native to the Midwest, and more earthy, innovative and exciting. Never having visited this part of the world, Turner innocently expected to see its regionalism reflected in every building he encountered, but what he found instead was the usual monotonous procession of farms and countryside, occasionally interrupted by gas stations and small towns.

When he first set eyes on Taliesin itself, however, his disappointment gave way to exuberance. Widely hailed as an exemplar for Wright's ideas about organic architecture, the great architect's homestead served partly as laboratory, partly as work in progress, and perhaps most important as a showcase of his work, meant to impress prospective clients. Although Turner had seen photographs of the fabled structure, and was well versed in its history, seeing the buildings with his own eyes in their actual setting was an unforgettable experience.

Turner had arrived at Taliesin planning to apply to be a student of Wright's, but quickly realized an apprenticeship would be too lengthy, too arduous and too fraught with powerful personalities—including, of course, that of Wright himself—to work to his advantage. Later, when he managed to secure the apprenticeship he sought with the master architect's son, John Lloyd Wright, Turner profited from a one-on-one working relationship with his chosen mentor. In marked contrast to his imperious and egocentric father, John Wright had a warm and giving personality that was reflected in his work. Turner grew to admire the way the younger Wright approached the needs of each new client as a singular architectural experience, yet every one of his buildings displayed a consistent grammar of construction that flowed throughout the structure. Although details might change with different uses, the building's basic grammar did not.

Turner, seeing through his sculptor's eyes, likened this grammar to that of a skeleton and its joints. The bones do not change but the tendons and the muscles do, creating a multitude of variations in form and movement. The relationship of the house to the land was also a critical element in John Lloyd Wright's design philosophy, and one that made an indelible impression on Turner's subsequent career.

An Evolving Philosophy of Sustainability

Turner's approach to design and architecture embodied the concept of sustainability long before the concept became fashionable within the contemporary green movement. His broader definition of sustainability includes not just environmental sustainability, but also social sustainability.

Turner defines his philosophy and approach to building design with a new term of his own, *terramonics*, which means living in harmony with the land. Turner's philosophy of terramonics is broader than the concerns of most environmentalists. It not only addresses the relationship of the building to the natural environment, but also puts at the center the need for creating a harmonious relationship for the human inhabitants to both their built and their natural environment. Examples of his terramonic design principles can be seen in all his projects, but most notably in the award-winning Park Place residences and Southfair office complex, both in Del Mar, California.

Elaborating on his terramonic principles, Turner states, "In industrialized society we have long lived with the idea of buildings conceived as separate structures, as objects set upon the land."

Buildings have traditionally been judged for their inherent stylistic qualities, but seldom for how well they were integrated with their environment. Even such architects as Frank Lloyd Wright, while applauded for their sensitivity to natural surroundings, are mainly discussed in terms of the beauty and drama of the built design. Terramonics reverses this process. The architect should first consider the land itself, and only then how the house will fit into the land around it. In the design of the site plan, Turner complains, too many designers install landscaping as an afterthought once the building itself is complete. Instead, Turner feels the architect must first determine an arrangement of the structure according to the topography, existing natural features, climatic orientation and vegetation so as to fully integrate the building into its site.

Second, Turner argues, to be truly sustainable, architecture must do more than just integrate into its setting according to a rigid doctrine of appropriate siting, use of renewable materials, energy conservation and other carefully planned design and construction features. To be truly sustainable, he believes, architecture must also take advantage of the particulars of a given site to create an optimal, supportive environment for the inhabitants.

Sustainability implies the ability to maintain worth and to endure over a period of time. In other words, buildings that are truly sustainable have an intrinsic worth that merits longevity. Further, Turner has realized, the most sustainable structures are those that not only are harmonious with the land, but also take advantage of all the assets of the site to create a habitable environment. Turner appreciates visually stimulating designs, but only when placed in the context of a wide-reaching philosophy of sustainability.

While deploring the destructive impact of much of conventional development, Turner simultaneously rejects narrow definitions of sustainability that advocate for environmental conservation but fail to take into account human values. On a practical level, he feels, a truly harmonious design encourages long-term stewardship by virtue of pride in a property and care for its maintenance. A truly harmonious design also respects a triad of factors that include the building itself, the land on which it is built (frequently neglected in modern development plans) and (even more frequently ignored) the people living or working there. While the inhabitants are unlikely to appreciate the finer points of an architectural design, they will readily demonstrate that they understand and embrace this basic principle of sustainability by simply staying put.

Creating a supportive environment for the inhabitants, ensuring that the people who live there are in harmony with both the house and the site in which it is located, is of paramount importance to Turner. Indeed, Herb Turner's central tenet of design is: "People who love their homes sustain them." His terramonic approach grew out of this maxim combined with an overarching environmental sensibility. And thus by creating houses and housing complexes that are loved and looked after by their owners, Turner enhances the social sustainability of his projects and helps to create vibrant, local communities.

Throughout his architectural career, Herb Turner has steered a middle course between two extremes—the shortsightedness of mainstream residential developers and the unreasonable demands of stringent environmentalists. On the one hand, he is dismayed by development that bulldozes large tracts of acreage, and then superimposes identical housing units on the landscape with no regard for their surroundings. On the other hand, as a developer, he has frequently found himself at odds with well-meaning environmental groups that focus solely on conserving the natural flora and fauna without regard for human needs and activities.

AL BOEKE ON THE SEA RANCH VISION FORTY YEARS LATER

The internationally renowned Sea Ranch is a special case of an expansive, sustainable community with significant architecture. Founded over forty years ago on the coast of northern California, the Sea Ranch stands out today as the premier model for environmentally sensitive residential design and construction, with a highly informed master plan for the care and stewardship of the spectacular natural environment, and homes carefully sited on the otherwise unaltered landscape.

In its first decade, the Sea Ranch enjoyed a heady period marked by a high degree of creativity that was achieved only at considerable expense. As word of the development's originality and excellence spread, coupled with an aggressive sales campaign, the novel community attracted a small group of enthusiastic residents who actively participated in its evolution. But in the decade that followed, a reaction set in, and the Sea Ranch suffered at the hands of a tidal wave of environmentalists and government zealots. They, by their own public statements, used Sea Ranch's reputation for excellence to leverage their bureaucratic incursion into California coastal development with the goal of statewide control by commission. In the process, this new generation of bureaucrats arrogantly and retroactively threw out years of private planning and county zoning, and millions of dollars in privately invested planning and infrastructure, radically constraining the original Sea Ranch development plans.

The Sea Ranch's third decade began ignominiously with bankruptcy, incurring legal fees of one million dollars apiece for the developer and the Sea Ranch community association, and resulting in the negation of county-approved planning and zoning that had been painstak-ingly and incrementally gained over years. The final blow came with the high-handed imposition of zoning restrictions that mandated exclusively single-family lots, thus contradicting the balanced range of single-family homes and condominiums that had been carefully planned. The opportunity to achieve the original commu-nal vision for the Sea Ranch, namely a diversified, mature, yet radically new kind of community, was thus irretrievably lost.

Today the original owners and members, along with an increasing number of new arrivals, find themselves enjoying an economic recovery, the emergence of the member association as a force in local government, and a rapid inflation of property values. On the one hand, the evolving model marks a radical change in the original

developer's goal of a community for "just plain folks" to one of an enclave for increasingly wealthier homeowners. Yet on the other hand, the result has been a rapidly growing community of several thousand residents who appreciate their good fortune and either don't care or aren't aware that Sea Ranch's founders have been deprived of their grand plan. It's the good life, yes, but sterilized by the intrusion of government into what could or should have been a phenomenal achievement.

Sea Ranch's fame, of course, derives largely from its architecture, which couldn't have come into being in its present form without strong planning guidelines. The development's core concept was indisputably its emphasis on the *commons,* a shared public space without private fences, although fenced enclosures were allowed for entryways, and for small patios and vegetable gardens. The carefully preserved public area made up fifty percent of the acreage and established an undivided interest among homeowners in the property's maintenance and repair. While it was taken for granted that as much of the existing vegetation as possible would be retained, the project's guidelines furthermore limited new plantings around buildings to indigenous species that wouldn't interfere with the project's rural effect.

Another key to the development's appeal lay in the designers' highly intuitive response to the area's existing wooden structures. The Sea Ranch's barnlike little houses were attractively grouped in a manner reminiscent of the hodgepodge of added-on outbuildings that had evolved on the neighborhood's working homesteads over the generations. Meanwhile their cedar siding could be expected to weather naturally in the same aesthetically pleasing fashion as the ramshackle buildings they replaced.

"Genetic variation" was provided by the contrasting personalities of the architectural design team. While the new structures adhered to a common formalist vocabulary of boldly geometric elevations and dramatic volumes, interiors provided room for further individuality, most notably expressed in playfully eccentric (and widely publicized) interiors by team partner Charles Moore. The iconoclastic exuberance of Moore, which is more prominent later in his career with formalist postmodern creations, gave the Sea Ranch design some of its most distinctive flair.

The Sea Ranch's resounding critical and financial success unfortunately could not help but draw the attention of the powers that be. The project had largely come about because of the close partnership between the developers and a local government that was not particularly choosy about the kind of development it attracted in an underdeveloped community. When the newly established California Coastal Commission started to involve itself in the details of the planning process however, the future direction of Sea Ranch was forever changed.

At a stroke, the Commission sabotaged a fundamental aspect of the project's objectives by eliminating the densely clustered condominiums for the remainder of the property. The Commission's belatedly imposed strictures virtually guaranteed that the rest of Sea Ranch would resemble those expensive tract developments that had begun springing up everywhere. The community, it is fair to say, never recovered its integrity after that, and today vast sections of the property are pockmarked by over-sized, awkwardly designed weekend mansions erected with negligible regard for their neighbors or their surroundings.

Although the original Sea Ranch vision was compromised, the bold ideas and new ways of thinking that characterized its development have made a mark in modern architecture, and inspired many architects and developers. The Sea Ranch is also home to a unique community of happy and proud residents.

On a Christmas day that commemorated forty years of the Sea Ranch, the following presentation was made to the Sea Ranch community, which had assembled in the "White Barn":

"Tonight, we Sea Ranchers are celebrating our past choices and our privileged future. Our best choice has allowed us to borrow this dynamic coastline as our home. We have created the means to expand our horizons as a self-governing and responsible, private community. The Sea Ranch Concept, whatever that was, has grown and matured into a dynamic Living Concept, a community of volunteers—women and men with wisdom, humor and gladness. The result is love of people as well as place, reflected in our faces as we understand and share. Our expansive lifestyle is contagious, going back to the future. Let us toast and join the ever-growing wave of creative self-starters who energize the richness and joy of our daily lives."

Al Boeke served as the lead developer of the Sea Ranch.

Turner contends that land *will* be developed for human habitat, and will continue to emphasize single-family homes in many areas. So why not improve upon this paradigm? Instead of evolving such commercial development options, the public is given only two extreme choices—either not to develop at all or to destroy natural landscapes to build poorly designed houses that constantly change ownership and consequently are detrimental to community vitality. Turner's Bernardo Mountain project in the San Diego area (see page 92) brought all these issues to the fore during his twenty-year struggle to develop what for him would have been a premier example of terramonic design: a stunning natural landscape preserved and celebrated with carefully designed and sited homes that would have no major impact on the environment. The project was finally lost in the mire of local politics—what Turner saw as ignorance on the part of bureaucrats who could not (or would not) understand terramonic design and an unreasonable no-growth attitude fomented by a few community members whom Turner saw as wrapping themselves in the banner of environmental protest.

While environmentalists have certainly played a key role in preserving natural systems and counteracting greedy developers who blatantly disregard the natural world, they have also discouraged intelligent green developments. Ironically, this often leads to low-quality sprawl. Turner also observes a disturbing trend on the part of American suburban communities over past decades: There are always noisy "nimby" coalitions who resist new development in their regions—Not In My Back Yard!—thus forcing developers to buy land for new communities ever farther out from urban centers.

The Terramonic Paradigm

Herb Turner's terramonic approach has become a paradigm, a new, integrated development model that emphasizes social as well as environmental sustainability. For Turner, sustainability still starts with *lifestyle*. He believes that a new sense of community can be developed with a well-preserved and well-lived-in natural environment as its common bond. Developing single-family residences is not just about building with ecological principles in mind, but also about designing homes that people will enjoy and sustain because they love them.

DEFINING TERRAMONIC

Terramonics is design that facilitates the harmonious integration of the house and the house-owners with the natural environment. Terramonics is *a way of thinking* as well as a design approach to home-building.

The Four Terramonic Processes

While theoretically it may be argued that the following four guidelines for terramonic design seem obvious, they actually present substantial challenge to the traditional way residential communities are developed.

Integrated Development Process

Vital to ideal terramonic development, a working dialogue including the designer, the builder and the resident produces a home that reflects the lifestyle and philosophy of its occupants. The people who will live in the buildings must be integrated into the development process, from conception to completion.

Land Planning

Terramonic land planning uses the topography and elements of the landscape to guide the general design of the project. Natural drainage, minimized grading and other design strategies preserve the natural environment, keeping as much water as possible on-site for native plants. Open space or park elements are provided for.

Environmental Design

Positioning individual structures in relation to the natural property contours assures both ecological integrity and fitting aesthetics. The natural environment is preserved and enhanced for low water usage and low maintenance. New but compatible species of plants may be introduced to subtly modify the native environment.

Residential Design

The natural terrain dictates the design of the house. The design process that fully utilizes the siting advantages creates a relationship between interior and exterior spaces so that residents are "living indoors while living outdoors." Custom plantings may be added close to the house, and interior plants can be used to contrast with the local landscape and to encourage interior-exterior communication and access.

In a totally terramonic house:

1) The architecture reflects care and concern for the lived experience of the inhabitants.

2) The architecture and the landscaping maximize the advantages offered by the site.

3) The building is integrated into and becomes part of the environment.

4) The building modulates shelter and privacy with exposure and openness.

There are four elements in the terramonics approach that distinguish it from the typical development process (see page 189). These elements are applicable to large multi-unit housing developments and, even more appropriately, to individual custom homes. In both cases the process encourages thorough dialogue between homeowners, the architect and the builder during the design phase. This assures that the eventual residents will be able to build a home that reflects their lifestyle, while also meeting Frank Lloyd Wright's ecological ideal as being "of the land not on the land."

Putting Philosophy Into Practice

Turner's philosophy of terramonics has evolved in the course of his career, starting with the influences of John Lloyd Wright and Al Boeke, the developer of the Sea Ranch. Project by project, Turner's development experiences grew, as did his firm belief that through an applied process the developer can resolve the conflict between sustainable development and the bureaucratic and commercial forces that resist it. Innovations, though often challenging to sell, permit and finance, can be realized with perseverance, and once proven are easier to repeat.

Over many decades and through many projects, Herb Turner's enthusiasm and thoughtful approach to his architectural craft have been very productive. His love of the Del Mar area, his regionalist sensibilities, his respect for the natural world and its processes, his inventive, pioneering character and his entrepreneurial zeal have all contributed to his success. For those who know the region's history, Herb Turner is recognized as one of the architects who distinctly shaped "Del Mar design"—that is, the contemporary lines, natural colors and materials, generous space and light, and landscape integration that characterize Del Mar's beautiful neighborhoods. He has also inspired, from the very beginning, a personal approach to homebuilding that integrates customized features meeting the individual needs of the homeowners with ecological sensitivity in the design, construction and ongoing maintenance of the property. Turner's higher ideals, which have not always been easy to put into practice, have driven his career.

When it comes to planning for a "green future," Turner's experiences have left him with both hope and dread. Like other astute observers, he sees the traditional homebuilding paradigm coming under increasing scrutiny as modern civilization comes to terms with its ecological and economic challenges. Everyone agrees that alternatives are essential, as the traditional models are not working. For Turner, alternative options are already available—they simply need to be adopted on a large scale. For example, terramonics answers many of the conservation concerns of the sustainable "green" movement. So why hasn't the so-called environmental movement developed a corresponding awareness that includes the human habitat? Furthermore, a "sustainable" design that ignores the context of its development fails to provide a truly terramonic solution. For example, a solar-heated home that is constructed by razing the vegetation and imposing a disruptive concrete pad on the property violates at least one basic tenet of such a philosophy. According to Turner, the current challenge is to educate and update the institutions that approve development plans, and broaden the public's awareness of the new sustainable community options available to them.

Turner is hopeful that his approach will be more widely embraced as homeowners and developers come to realize that truly sustainable modern settlements need to be designed and lived in according to essential human-centered factors. For Turner, the sustainable approach to home-building includes and preserves the natural ecology—from the vision of the design, through the building and remodeling processes, through decades of inspired stewardship and healthy, happy *living* in a home harmoniously integrated with its environment over time.

Toward Green Development

"*Developers can promote sustainable development by pursuing a real-world process that integrates the built environment with the natural environment and that uses modern technology to enhance traditional development approaches. Yet, an emphasis on sustainable qualities of development need not require developers to sacrifice profitability.*

"*Both collaboration and whole-systems thinking in approaching development will allow developers to realize more sustainable relationships with their constituent public officials and consumer markets, more sustainable support from envi-*

ronmental and other interest groups, and more sustainable returns, in monetary and fulfillment terms, from their professional pursuits."
—Douglas R. Porter, *The Practice of Sustainable Development*

Slow but steady progress is being made in the mainstream development industry. The U. S. Green Building Council has developed new standards for rating homes and other buildings. Their LEED (Leadership in Energy and Environmental Design) Green Building Rating System of sustainability factors is becoming widely adopted. High-profile commercial developments with advanced green design features, such as The Henry condominium high-rise in Portland, Oregon has been a noteworthy financial success. Today, being "green" sells. The public is increasingly aware of the need for ecological sustainability and is responsive to well-thought-out alternatives when it comes time to choose or build a home. The corporate world is getting on board as well, with major companies such as Coca-Cola and IBM creating signature "green" corporate centers and manufacturing plants.

While these positive trends give Turner hope, he remains deeply concerned about the bureaucratic and often grossly out-of-touch political approval process that developers face when they attempt to innovate in response to environmental concerns. The inertia of old ways, often reinforced by politicized local power structures with "not invented here" or "leave well enough alone" syndromes, resists evolutionary directions. Very often, the authority to make major decisions is left to underqualified, ill-informed and unmotivated bureaucrats whose personal whims determine the fate of major development initiatives and consequently of the environment.

Adding to his concern is the fact that politicians and bureaucrats are not interested in being educated about alternative principles. As a case in point, Turner contrasts the experience of speaking to university audiences with appearing before the conclaves that are part of the approval process for building. When he conveys his experiences and ideas for terramonic development to the former group, those gathered are almost universally interested and very positive. They ask questions, they contribute useful ideas—they empower him to do his work. On the other hand, in almost every instance of a Coastal Commission review or a local zoning authority permit hearing, he and his team are given ten minutes to present an hour's worth of material. Unconventional solutions are most often struck down, by bureaucrats who don't have the education to fully understand and appreciate the concepts being presented. The established point of view prevails, even if it is woefully simplistic and out of date, until it is chiseled away over months or years, circumvented or somehow overcome so that a new perspective can arise on the long-term requirements for sustainable

IMPORTANT FACTORS IN TURNER'S APPROACH TO GREEN ARCHITECTURE INCLUDE DESIGNING ON A HUMAN SCALE AND INTEGRATING THE ENCLOSED LIVING SPACE WITH THE NATURAL SURROUNDINGS.

193

development. Turner hopes that public sentiment and economic necessity will force lawmakers and civic agencies to radically update their approach and open the doors for widespread green innovations in commercial and residential real-estate developments.

At present, Herb Turner continues to develop new projects, and is increasingly interested in the green architecture and sustainable community movements, which are finally maturing as methodologies, market conditions and politics address new solutions on many levels. A sea change is coming, and Turner looks forward with hope and excitement to the positive innovations that will bring about a new harmony between human communities and the natural world.

Turner sees potential in today's "green architecture movement" for reversing the constraints that have been forced upon developers by shortsighted "no growthers" of the past. "There is no avoiding the fact that housing will be built as the population continues to grow," says Turner. "So we need a revolution not only in how we build but in how we live."

Given a fair chance, developers will respond to people's desire to live a green lifestyle, and Turner is confident that the marketplace will encourage the systemic changes needed in the development industry for truly green development to occur.

"A balance of housing density and a healthy, accessible natural environment is what everyone really wants and needs. Building with an environmental, or green, awareness certainly means designing and siting in harmony with the land," says Turner.

But to truly create and sustain a home with heart and *a sense of place*, he asserts, "People need to enjoy and take pride in the whole environment, to be sensitive to all its aspects—built and natural—and to make the most of what they have to work with. It's really quite simple: Enjoying one's home and being a steward of the environment, in whatever form it takes, is the key."

Turner points out that a better quality of life and green awareness come together when one makes informed and creative choices. "Green can mean refurbishing an historic property, planting a communal garden with suburban neighbors, going 'off the grid' for electricity or investing in a planet-friendly urban home in the city instead of the latest gas-guzzling, isolated bedroom community 45 miles out I-70!"

As Herb Turner's own life and work have exemplified, consciously shaping integrated lifestyles is how people will influence the evolution, over time, of a wholly sustainable *human* environment.

THE VICTORY
OF THE TRUTH
IS CERTAIN

Herb Turner on Rodin's "Testament"

Because Auguste Rodin's "Testament for the Young Artist" was one of the most important influences in the development of Herb Turner's approach to all aspects of his art—not only sculpture, but also painting and architecture—Turner's translation of the "Testament" appears in full on pages 42 and 43 in Chapter 1, "Finding a Voice." This Appendix presents Turner's commentary on Rodin's life and times, and on the value of the "Testament" for artists today.

Students and artists, in their search for knowledge, desire to find writings by the great artists of the past to help them in their aspirations. Generally, artists, outside of the literary field, are devoted to their chosen profession so that they do not make the effort to describe their philosophy for future generations. Therefore they leave us only their artistic achievements as a teaching medium. Probably natural reticence about their own work makes writing to an unknown and apparently uninspired public, difficult. Then again, the energy needed to enter the foreign field of writing saps energy from their prime mission.

The unfortunate result of this phenomenon is that writing on art is left to critics who do not practice the craft. Consequently, authentic information from artists of the past is rare, and furthermore, difficult to find when one is confronted with the vast amount of material that has been written by others.

Since the source material is extremely limited to critics writing on the practice of art, we wonder how so much can be written on the subject. The contention must be that much is manufactured by critics, or comes from other sources than those gained through actual experience. Consequently, it is encouraging as well as exciting when one discovers authentic and unknown works by great artists.

It was my teacher, Mr. Naum Los, who introduced me to the works of Auguste Rodin and to the method of teaching that Mr. Los had derived from Horace Lecoq de Boisbaudran, Rodin's teacher.

Mr. Los instructed me to find my master and to study his early work. For it is in a master's early work that a student can discover how he became a master. Then if one is really determined, one should study the work of the master's teacher, if one can find out who he was and what he thought. So I felt doubly blessed in that Mr. Los had studied both Rodin and Lecoq before he came to this country by invitation of the federal government.

Enamored as I was of Rodin, I asked Mr. Los for material on Rodin and he recommended that I read Paul Gsell's conversations with Rodin as they had been translated into English. I read this book with great enthusiasm for I had always been looking for words directly from the artist unencumbered by the interpretation of others.

Once, Mr. Los asked me to lend him my English translation of Gsell so that he could compare it to the original French edition. To our mutual surprise, Mr. Los realized that the French edition had an additional chapter that I believe was called "Testament for the Young Artist."

I immediately became very interested in discovering what this particular chapter contained, as I thought it would reveal something important to me. I asked Mr. Los if he would translate it for me. He declined for he felt that this was an important writing that would have more meaning to me if I myself translated it. He volunteered to review my translation. I laboriously translated this chapter, a bit at a time, and Mr. Los reviewed it.

A few years later, while I was studying architecture with John Lloyd Wright, the architect son of Frank Lloyd Wright, in Del Mar, California, the "Testament" surfaced again during a discussion about teachers and teaching methods.

During one of my frequent discussions with John Lloyd Wright and his wife, Frances, I mentioned the innovative teaching of Lecoq and how the architect Eugene Emmanuel Viollet-le-Duc was supportive of his teaching methods. Frances Wright immediately became interested. This interest led to my mentioning my translation of Rodin's "Testament," which I produced for her review.

Frances Wright immediately recognized the value of the "Testament" and suggested she and I endeavor to get it published. She thought it was a valuable work as it validated the same principles of form and space seen in the work of architects from Viollet-le-Duc to Louis Sullivan to Frank Lloyd Wright—that is, the principles of organic architecture. Since these principles were validated in another art form, namely sculpture, it further validated the theory that these were basic universal principles and that the understanding of these principles was essential to the creation not only of art but of life itself.

With this motivation I wrote a foreword to the "Testament" with the goal of publishing the apparently unknown writing of Rodin. The effort to publish it, however, was in vain. It is a matter of great pleasure to be able to see the "Testament" published now in this book.

Although this testament (on pages 42 and 43) can be readily appreciated by artists and laymen alike, I believe additional information on Rodin's background would be beneficial. I have not attempted to give a complete history of Rodin's life, but have chosen those parts pertinent in understanding the qualities that formed this testament.

For any country to have produced an extraordinary genius like Rodin is a marvel in itself, but when one realizes his poverty-stricken birthright, it is even a greater cause for wonder. Rodin was born in 1840. During his early school training he showed little promise, for after several years he was almost illiterate. This apparent indifference to scholastics is accounted for by his nearsightedness, which made it impossible for him to see the classroom blackboard. This ignorance was overcome later in life through extensive individual study. He did, however, at this time acquire a desire to draw and apparently he excelled at it.

In 1854, before Rodin was able to finish his studies, he was obliged to leave school to learn a trade. When he informed his family that he wished to learn to draw, his father opposed the idea, but later consented to let him attend École Impériale de Dessin, commonly called the Petite École. Here, his father hoped, his son would make practical use of his gifts.

It was at this early stage that he came under the influence of Horace Lecoq de Boisbaudran, one of the most inspired teachers of his day. Most of the great artists of the previous generation had benefited from Lecoq's tutelage. In Rodin's generation there were also the sculptor Jules Dalou, the etcher Alphonse Legros, the painter Henri Fantin-Latour and the medalist Jules-Clement Chaplain. In the Petite École, Lecoq was in a fortunate position to strongly influence the minds of unaffected youths before they faced the academic École des Beaux-Arts training.

To understand the influence in the Petite École, one must study Lecoq's teachings, which are available to us in L. D. Luard's translation of Lecoq's

Training of the Memory in Art. In order to appreciate the advanced thinking of Lecoq, one must understand that Beaux-Arts education was a slavish worship of the antiques of the past, and success here was measured in prizes, of which the supreme reward was the "Grand Prix de Rome." Lecoq, in describing this situation and aftermath, states:

> The young people who enter for these competitions, to be sure, are carefully exhibited as examples that point to the true road to success.
>
> Is the full effect of such misdirection understood even yet? Do people really see how it leads most of the competitors to reject all ideas and inspiration of their own and to servilely copy such work as the school holds up to honor, which it consecrates by success?
>
> I ask all who have been at the École des Beaux-Arts, is this not what generally happens? And sadder still, are not the students often heard to say that if they are trying to imitate the manner and style of such and such a prize work, it is not because they admire it? They admit that they are perfectly aware they are taking a direction quite opposite to their own taste and real artistic feeling, but mean later to become themselves again, once the prize is won. But an artist's conviction is a religious faith, which cannot stoop to such sordid calculations without a sort of apostasy.
>
> The harm would not be beyond all cure if the young competitor only carried off the "grand prix" at first attempt. But who can hope for such good luck? The pursuit of the Grand Prix de Rome always absorbs an artist for many years, if not the whole of the artist's youth. With scarcely an exception, no student succeeds even in being admitted to compete for this prize—that is, he does not reach what is called the "entree en loge"—until he has spent some years working exclusively to this end. It is the length of time spent in this way that works against his chance of retaining his originality.
>
> Pupils who spend all their time at this competition end up like certain students who are trying for a degree by caring much more for getting their diploma than for acquiring a knowledge of their subject.
>
> Two tests must be passed before one is admitted "en loge": a sketch or composition of a given subject and a figure painted from nature. To practice for these tests then, becomes the student's whole preoccupation. Every day he devotes himself exclusively to making routine compositions and studies of the figure, always on the scale, and within the prescribed time limits, carefully copying the examination style.
>
> After whole years devoted to such practice, what can be left of the student's most precious qualities? Of his naivete, his sincerity, his naturalness? The exhibitions of École des Beaux-Arts give us only too clear an answer.

Some of the competitors imitate the style of their master or some other well-known artist. Others try to copy the work of recent prizewinners, the last exhibition hit, or any picture that has recently struck them. Such different influences may give an exhibition an apparent variety, but it is very different from the real variety and originality that comes from personal inspiration.

Let us admit at once that often much of the work shows real talent and skill; but what one does not find are just the qualities one would expect to find most in young people's work—and they are the most interesting qualities, too, and those that show the greatest promise for the future—namely, spontaneity, go, naivete, freshness of impression; in a word, the qualities of youth!

What can be the reason for a state of things so general and so unnatural, if it is not a system opposed to the free development of individuality?

I have pointed out some of the evils that belong to competitions, but there are others no less serious; for competitions accustom the students to overlook the nobler and purer pleasure that is found in the pursuit of beauty, in a search for praise and self-advancement. . . .

The classical school, which unceasingly extols beauty and the pursuit of beauty, always speaks of it as having already attained its climax of absolute and final expression in works of the past. Now beauty is not exclusively Greek or Roman. All aspects of nature, even the most ordinary, possess a certain beauty of their own. The artist's business is to discover and make plain to others the finer point of view of scenes of every kind, to disentangle their dominant characteristics and to express with emphasis the artistic sentiment that underlies them.

In direct contradiction to the Beaux-Arts education was Lecoq's teaching:

An artist, in the highest sense of the word, is inspired by a passionate love of beauty; he is a true lover of nature and does not see her imperfections, but discovers beauties that escape the eye of the ordinary observer. These he combines and idealizes in his work, impressing them with the stamp of his own personality. All artists have observed nature with the same sincerity, according to their instinctive preferences. Each one of them has also learned how to execute his works so as to affect us powerfully with the impression that it was given to him alone to receive. By showing us some personal view of nature, by giving us some fresh interpretation of her, or some idealized conception that she has inspired, by showing her as strong and terrible or gentle and sublime, these masters raise us to a higher plane of thought. They charm and refresh us, increasing in number and variety our store of exquisite and nobler enjoyments. The least among them has his use and takes his place of right in the chain of art, for his absence would mean the loss of a link.

Art then, when understood in its widest sense, consists not only of higher manifestations, but of all manifestations that bear the mark of passionate and individual conviction. Innumerable and magnificent as such manifestations have been in the past, there is yet an inexhaustible store of them in the future, for the shades and variety of human feeling from which they spring are infinite in number and always fresh and new.

From this we may, I think, logically deduce the following maxims: "Art is essentially individual—it is individuality that makes the artist an artist."

From which consequently results a second formula: "All teaching, that is real teaching, based upon reason and good sense, must aim to keep the artist's individual feeling pure and unspoiled, to cultivate it and bring it to perfection."

As for his classroom teaching, we have accounts from Henri Fantin-Latour's letters. Luard, in his translation, relates: "They describe Lecoq's teaching as always very simple. They show how careful he was to take into account each student's individual temperament and give him the particular counsel that he felt was best suited to his needs at the moment. He very rarely took up brush or charcoal when criticizing his pupils' studies and never allowed them to see his own work, for fear they should be led into imitation."

Fantin-Latour tells of the expeditions into the country that he and his fellows made upon Sundays—often to the pond at Villebon—where they bathed and made memory studies of each other in the open air; of how they discovered on the outskirts of Paris an inn with a high-walled garden, where Lecoq subsequently organized classes for working from the model outdoors—a great innovation in those days. One can see from Fantin-Latour's description that Lecoq was one of the early advocates of the "plein air" painting of the Impressionists.

Lecoq developed a unique system of graduate exercises to train the students' visual memory to a point never before attained. One of the pupils said of the first lesson he had from him:

> Lecoq sat me down to copy an engraving. When I showed him the result, confident that I did rather well and expecting him to praise me, he took out a penknife and with its point showed me where I had failed in really giving

the line of the back, of the foot and other parts. I set to work again, determined this time to win the approval that had been withheld.

"Better," was his comment, "but still not exact enough," and again the penknife relentlessly pointed out the inaccuracies. Five times I had to make the drawings before he was satisfied.

The camera was being developed and many people believed that it would eliminate artistic representation. To this Lecoq replied:

> Truth in art is not photographic truth, as many people seem to think nowadays. Numbers of painters seem, under the influence of this idea, to be entering into a rivalry with the camera, as laborious as it is futile. I grant that in the direction of detail and illusion they have achieved results such as the old masters neither dreamed of nor tried for. Yet to appreciate this triumph of the moderns at its proper value, let us suppose for a moment that photography were to succeed one day in reproducing and fixing color. In that case where would the most detailed and most successful imitation be in comparison with pictures of nature that were similar to a reflection in a looking glass? The works of great masters, such as Titian, Raphael, Michelangelo and others, would not lose by comparison with the mechanical pictures of photography, but would appear all the finer. What makes real art would then be far better understood and it would be admitted beyond question that *art is not just nature*, but it is *the interpretation of nature through human feeling and human genius*.

As a final proof of Lecoq's ability, we have Rodin's statement, "I have retained most of what he taught me. At that time, Legros and the rest of the youngsters did not realize, as I do now, our good fortune in coming under the influence of such a teacher."

It was at the Petite École that Rodin decided to become a sculptor and devoted all his time to study. He arose early, and dawn found him in the studio of Lauset, ready for work. From eight o'clock until noon he studied at the Petite École. In the afternoon he drew from the antiques at the Louvre, or went to the Bibliotheque Imperiale and studied drawings from albums of Michelangelo and Raphael. In the evenings he followed the practice advocated by Lecoq and drew from memory those things which impressed him most during the day. Rodin's extreme poverty forced this intense work upon him, and this poverty, which was his companion until he was fifty, served him well.

After three years at the Petite École, at the age of seventeen, Rodin's formal training there came to an end. Rodin now hoped to be able enter the École des Beaux-Arts, which was considered by most people to be the only school for the education of the artist. Although Rodin was thought of by his fellow students as possessing great talent, he was steeped in traditions contrary to those advocated by the Beaux-Arts and was refused on three separate attempts. This was his first of many rebuffs by the politically powerful academicians.

Rodin was forced to give up his formal studies to work in allied trades as an ornament worker, a sculptor's caster and a model maker. But he found time to draw at the museum and to study anatomy at the École de Medicine and at the anatomical museum.

One day in the workshop, the inexperienced Rodin was helpfully criticized by an older colleague: "You're doing it wrong. Don't have your leaves lying flat. They look dull, like bas-reliefs. Turn up the edges; that will look like sculpture." This statement pointed out clearly to Rodin the great principle of sculpture that his art exemplifies so well—to think of sculpture in depth, with elements reaching outward to create bigger shadows, and not as a carving out of a flat plane.

By the time Rodin was twenty he had secured his livelihood by working in the studios of Albert-Ernest Carrier-Belleuse and was able to afford a stable that he used for a studio. Here he worked on a large figure for two years, but unfortunately it was destroyed by careless handling when he moved.

Rodin modeled a bust of an old man, which he considered to be executed well enough to be exhibited at the Salon of 1864. But the bust cracked due to his inability to keep the stable-studio properly heated. Only the mask was left. Still determined, Rodin had this fragment cast and sent it to the Salon. It was refused. The bust, now called *L' Homme au Nez Casse*, can be seen in some of the great museums throughout the world.

The war of 1870 forced Rodin into the army, but he was soon discharged because of his poor eyesight. Carrier-Belleuse, now in Belgium, heard that Rodin was free from service without means of livelihood, so he sent for him. Rodin, now thirty, left for Carrier-Belleuse's studio where he intended to work for several months. It was six years before he saw Paris again.

Rodin soon quarreled with Carrier-Belleuse and lost his position. The privations of war and its aftermath left his family in dire straits. But for the help of a few friends, he would not have had money for food. In a letter to Rose Beuret, Rodin said, "No work for almost three months, and you can imagine what a hard time it's been. There has been a quarrel with M. Carrier, but things are better now. A chemist here and also one of my colleagues have helped me. Without them I cannot imagine what would have happened. I asked you, in that long letter I wrote, to pawn my trousers; that would be money easily earned."

Carrier-Belleuse eventually returned to Paris, and Antoine Van Rasbourg, his assistant, took over his work in Brussels. Van Rasbourg and Rodin entered into a partnership that lasted five years.

Rodin further wrote to Rose in 1871, "I can spend almost nothing, because we are not paid immediately for our work. Not long ago I had a meal of ten centimes' worth of mussels and the same of fried potatoes. It's been like another siege. How I dream of buying a whole ham, but though my luck has changed, the money is still to come."

Through those years in Belgium, Rodin was apparently unconcerned with fame or fortune, but worked to acquire the slow, sure mastery of his art.

The climax of his stay in Brussels was casting his first important life-size statue. Rodin threw all his energies into this work. Before starting his statue, Rodin went to Italy, traveling and living as cheaply as possible. From Florence, he wrote to Rose, "You will not be surprised when I tell you that the moment I arrived in Florence I began to study Michelangelo, and I believe the great magician is going to reveal some of his secrets to me. But none of his pupils or his masters could do what he did, and I don't understand that; I have analyzed the work of his actual pupils. The secret was his and his alone. I've made sketches in the evenings in my room, not of his works, but figures that I've imagined and elaborated in order to understand his technique. Well, I think I have succeeded in discovering that quality, that nameless something which he alone could give."

Years later, in 1906, Rodin wrote further of Michelangelo's influence on him, "Michelangelo liberated me from academic methods. In teaching me (by observation) rules that were diametrically opposed to the ones I have been taught (School of Ingress), he set me free. . . . He held out his powerful hand to me and helped me over the bridge from one school to the other. This mighty Geryon carried me across."

After his trip to Italy, Rodin was fired by the inspiration he gained from Michelangelo's work and upon his return was more determined than ever to excel. The journey to Italy had convinced him that he was taking the right course. Michelangelo, whom Rodin so justly credits, showed him that the secret lay in the vigor of the modeling and that this study lay in the human body itself. He now realized that what he had gone to Rome and Florence to find was in his own studio.

His friendship with a Belgian soldier led to the latter posing for the endless sittings needed to complete his work. "One must not be in a hurry . . . an artist's reputation can be made with one statue," was Rodin's creed, and it sustained him for the eighteen months that he worked on this one statue.

This statue, now called *L'Age d'Airain*, was first exhibited in Brussels, where it was met with praise but also with derogatory insinuations: "M. Rodin, one of our talented sculptors who has heretofore been represented in the Salon by his busts only, shows at the Cercle Artistique a statue destined to figure at the Exposition de Paris.

"It will not pass unnoticed here, for it not only attracts one's attention on account of its strangeness but holds that attention on account of a precious and rare quality: life.

"We cannot discuss here how much casting direct from the human body there is in it; we merely wish to mention the figure whose appearance of physical and mental collapse is so expressively portrayed—we have no other information than that supplied by the work itself—that the sculptor seems to us to have endeavored to represent a man about to commit suicide."

Although Rodin refuted these damaging accusations, they continued to spread. The work was sent to the Salon of 1877 in Paris, where it was exhibited. However, the accusations that it was a clever casting from life began to mount to the point where the statue was in danger of being excluded from the exhibition.

Shaken and depressed by this scandal, Rodin requested an inquiry by the undersecretary for the Bureau of Fine Arts. Unfortunately the committee appointed by the undersecretary was composed of art critics and writers who possessed neither the ability to judge the statue nor the courage to oppose the Salon jury. Their statement, "The committee is not convinced that there has been any falsification," forced Rodin to protest to the undersecretary, who advised him to have castings and photographs made from the model who posed. This was done at Rodin's expense. Unfortunately, the cases sent were never opened.

Through these discouraging days, Rodin continued to work for various decorative sculptors to earn his living and to pay for the additional expense of his battle for honest judgment of his statue. One day a young sculptor, Alfred Boucher, came upon Rodin working in Laoust's studio. Boucher was amazed at the rapidity and skill of execution of this sculptor, and asked his name. Upon hearing it was Rodin, whom the art world was calling a counterfeit, he went to the sculptor Paul Dubois on Rodin's behalf. Dubois brought his friend, Henri-Michel-Antoine Chapu to the studio, where Rodin executed some work which convinced them of his sincerity and ability. These men obtained the support of several other established sculptors and addressed a letter to the undersecretary telling of Rodin's sincerity of execution and that this artist was destined to become a great sculptor in France. Chapu, Dubois, Carrier-Belleuse, Eugene Delaplanche, Falgiere and Thomas signed this letter. This act cleared the air and brought Rodin's name and work to the attention of more people than would have heard it had he won first prize.

When Rodin was thirty-nine, he again found employment with Carrier-Belleuse, this time at Sevres, a suburb of Paris, and continued to work there for three years. Although Rodin had produced such great works as *L' Age d'Airain* and *St. John the Baptist Preaching*, he was still forced to do the work of the artisan to earn his living.

As time passed, Rodin found a few devoted followers interested in his work. One such person was M. Turquet of the Ministry of Fine Arts, who secured him for a commission to do a monumental door of high decorative character. With this commission, the state allotted a studio to Rodin, which he was allowed to keep for the remainder of his life.

Rodin received 30,000 francs for the commission, which would have been a fortune to the average sculptor, but his consuming desire to produce a masterpiece, and the twenty years he would work on *La Porte de l'Enfer*, made the sum unimportant. The state further had to advance 35,000 francs to have it cast, but then revoked the commission. Rodin was obliged to pay back all the money received and kept *La Porte de l'Enfer* until his death, when he bequeathed it to the state.

An indefatigable worker, Rodin would be up at six and at work by seven, and would sometimes carry on his labor at night by candlelight. *La Porte de l'Enfer* included 186 figures, and was over twenty feet high and eight feet wide. In later years Rodin was to draw upon the figures in this door for many of his famous statues.

No work of a similar nature had ever been produced for several hundred years, and when exhibited, it received the acclaim of press and public alike. With this work Rodin attracted to himself a small band that devotedly supported and defended him.

In the midst of other activities, Rodin learned that the city of Calais wished to erect a monument to honor its heroic citizens, who, in the fourteenth century, had offered their lives to the King of England in order to save the besieged city from destruction. Rodin was immediately interested and familiarized himself with the subject's history by reading old chronicles and historical writings.

Through a friend in Calais, Rodin was able to invite the mayor and chairman of the commission, M. Omer Dewavrin, to his studio in Paris. The mayor was so convinced that "he almost gave me the order for the monuments, but he never asked other sculptors to submit maquettes." Rodin took the whole of autumn 1884 to work at a rough model of the sculpture. In a letter to M. Dewavrin in January 1885, Rodin writes: "Since receiving your honored visit, I have been applying myself to the monument and I have been lucky enough to hit upon an idea that I like, and which will be original when executed; I have seen nowhere any arrangement so suited to its subject or one that will be so absolutely appropriate. It will be all the better because all the other cities usually have the same monument, except for minor details. . . . What I have sent is merely a suggestion of the thoughts I will express, but the arrangement of a group of six figures appealed to me at once, for I knew what sameness there is in all monuments to great men."

Rodin named this group of six figures *Les Bourgeois de Calais*. Rodin wrote of his expectations to Alphonse Legros, who in turn informed the painter, Jean-Charles Cazin. All three of these artists had been students together at the Petite École under Lecoq de Boisbaudran. Legros and Cazin visited the mayor of Calais to see the model, and both artists were enthusiastic about the work.

In January 1885, Rodin appeared before the commission to defend his project and explain it in detail. His faith in the idea convinced the committee, and a mutual agreement was signed for its execution.

At the end of July, Rodin sent a second model (in which the figures were twenty-two inches high) for acceptance by the committee before he proceeded to execute the final work, which was to be six-and-one-half feet high. Because of the originality of the work, Rodin expected some opposition, as can be seen in a letter to the secretary of the committee.

Rodin wrote: "Will you kindly send me the committee's comment. I hope I am not to be bothered too much with alterations. You know the danger of disturbing the harmony of a piece of sculpture; it is like a tragedy or an opera—you take something away and the whole work is thrown out of proportion; then months of work are required to recapture the balance. It is not that I am afraid of work, but I have developed my project so carefully—it has taken me five months—that if I have to repeat this labor, much time will be lost and I am not likely to hit upon a better idea."

Rodin's fears were well-founded, as the secretary's reply shows: "We did not visualize our glorious fellow-citizens proceeding to the King of England's camp in this way. Their dejected attitudes offend our religion. . . . The silhouette of the group leaves much to be desired in the way of elegance. . . . We feel bound to insist that M. Rodin shall undertake to alter the positions of his figures and the silhouette of the group as a whole."

Rodin's strong commitment to his principle can be seen in his reply: "If the heads were to form a pyramid (the Louis David method) instead of a cube—straight lines—I would be following the dictates of scholastic principles to which I am absolutely opposed. They have been prevalent in our century and are in complete contradiction to the great epochs of the art of the past, and they give works conceived under their influence a cold lifeless conventionality. . . . I am the enemy in Paris of this pompous and scholastic kind of art. You want me to be a follower of people whose conventional style I despise. . . . The cube gives me the expression I want; the cone is a hobbyhorse of students competing for the Prix de Rome."

Through the combined efforts of M. Dewavrin, chairman of the committee, and of the sculptor Jean-Paul Laurens, who came to Rodin's aid, the committee authorized Rodin to proceed with the work.

The committee was not accustomed to Rodin's slow, patient execution and so became uneasy at delays, which they could not understand. To this Rodin replied: "Sculptors who are commissioned to execute monuments nowadays are not given enough time and their work is, without exception, bad. Many of them cast from life; that is, they produce photographic work; that kind goes quickly, but it is not art."

The time element was soon eliminated when a financial calamity in Calais swallowed up part of the funds for the monument. In view of the lack of money, some Calais citizens suggested the erection of one of "les Bourgeois de Calais." Annoyed by this, Rodin said to his friends one day, "The Calais Municipal Council would like to have one 'Bourgeois,' but it doesn't want six. . . . The group got in my way at the studio and I had to rent a stable for it in the rue Saint Jacques. . . . 'Les Bourgeois de Calais' must wait in a stable till their fate is decided."

Finally in June 1895, eleven years after its conception, the monument, in its entirety, was erected in Calais.

* * * *

Other details of Rodin's life are vitally interesting and can be read in Judith Cladel's book, *Rodin: The Man and His Art*.

RESOURCES ON PAINTING, SCULPTURE AND ARCHITECTURE

This section offers a wealth of reading (and visual) resources that have proved instructive and inspirational for Herb Turner. The list is divided into three main sections—"Painting," "Sculpture" and "Architecture"— followed by a "Miscellaneous" section with two important references.

PAINTING
Artists (listed alphabetically by surname)

George Bellows: The Artist and His Lithographs, 1916–1924. Linda Ayres and Jane E. Myers. Amon Carter Museum. Fort Worth, Texas. 1988.

Thomas Hart Benton: An American Original. Nelson Gallery Foundation. Alfred Knopf. New York. 1989.

Charles Burchfield. Mather Baigell. Watson-Guptill Publications. New York. 1976.

Gustave Caillebotte. Kirk Varnedoe. Yale University Press. New Haven, Connecticut. 1987.

Degas. Robert Gordon and Andrew Forge. Harry N. Abrams, Inc. New York. 1996.

Harvey Dinnerstein: Artist at Work. Harvey Dinnerstein. Watson-Guptill Publications. New York. 1978.

Thomas Eakins. Lloyd Goodrich. Harvard University Press. Cambridge, Massachusetts. 1982.

Eakins Watercolors. Donelson Hoopes. Watson-Guptill Publications. New York. 1985.

Nicolai Fechin. Mary Balcomb. Northland Publishing. Flagstaff, Arizona. 1985.

Childe Hassam. Donelson F. Hoopes. Watson-Guptill Publications. New York. 1988.

Robert Henri and His Circle. William I. Homer. Hacker Art Books. New York. 1988.

Winslow Homer. Lloyd Goodrich. George Braziller, Inc. New York. 1959.

Edward Hopper. Lloyd Goodrich. Harry N. Abrams, Inc. New York. 1993.

Peter Hurd: A Portrait Sketch from Life. Paul Horgan. University of Texas Press. Austin, Texas. 1965.

George Inness and the Visionary Landscape. Adrienne Baxter Bell. George Braziller, Inc. New York. 2003.

Eastman Johnson: Painting America. Teresa Carbone *et al.* Brooklyn Museum. Brooklyn, New York. 1999.

Manet, 1832–1883. Charles S. Moffet. Harry N. Abrams, Inc. New York. 1984.

Reginald Marsh. Lloyd Goodrich. Harry N. Abrams, Inc. New York. 1973.

Mathews: Masterpieces of the California Decorative Style. Harvey L. Jones. Gibbs Smith, Publisher. Layton, Utah. 1972.

Renoir. Walter Pach. Kessinger Publishing. Whitefish, Montana. 2004.

John Singer Sargent. Carter Ratliff. Abbeville Press. New York. 2001.

The Painter: Joaquin Sorolla y Bastida. Edmund Peel. Philip Wilson Publishers. London. 1989.

Moses Soyer: A Human Approach. Moses Soyer. ACA Galleries. New York. 1972.

Raphael Soyer—Paintings and Drawings. Walter Gutman. Shoewood Publishing Co. New York. 2006.

Toulouse-Lautrec. Edouard Julien. Crown Publishing Group. New York. 1985.

Robert Vickrey: Artist at Work. Robert Vickrey. Watson-Guptill Publications. New York. 1979.

Unknown Terrain: The Landscapes of Andrew Wyeth. Beth Venn *et al.* Whitney Museum of American Art. New York. 1998.

Andrew Wyeth: The Helga Pictures. John Wilmerding. Harry N. Abrams, Inc. New York. 1992.

Periods and Schools of Art

After the Hunt: William Harnett and Other American Still Life Painters, 1870–1900. Alfred Frankenstein. University of California Press. Berkeley, California. 1975.

American Art of Our Century. Lloyd Goodrich, John Baur. Fredrick Praeger, Publisher. New York. 1961.

The American Century: Art and Culture 1900–1950. Barbara Haskell. W. W. Norton. New York. 1999.

American Expressionism: Art and Social Change 1920–1950. Bram Dijkstra. Harry N. Abrams, Inc. New York. 2003.

American Impressionism and Realism: The Painting of Modern Life, 1885–1915. H. Barbara Weinberg. Metropolitan Museum of Art. New York. 1994.

American Impressionists Abroad and at Home: Paintings from the Collection of the Metropolitan Museum of Art. H. Barbara Weinberg *et al.* American Federation of Arts. New York. 2001.

American Painting, from the Armory Show to the Depression. Milton W. Brown. Princeton University Press. Princeton, New Jersey. 1955.

American Realism. Edward Lucie-Smith. Harry N. Abrams, Inc. New York. 1994.

Paintings of California. S. I. F. Fort. University of California Press. Berkeley, California. 1997.

Painting Technique

The Artist's Handbook of Materials and Techniques. Ralph Mayer. Penguin Group. New York. 1991.

Gist of Art: Principle and Practice Expounded in the Classroom and Studio. John Sloan. Dover Publications. New York. 2000.

Magic Realist Painting Techniques. Rudy de Reyna. Watson-Guptill Publications. New York. 1973.

The Materials of the Artist and Their Use in Painting: With Notes on the Techniques of the Old Masters. Max Doerner. Harcourt Trade Publishers. San Diego, California. 1949.

Methods and Materials of Painting of the Great Schools and Masters. Charles L. Eastlake. Dover Publications. New York. 2001.

Milk and Eggs: The American Revival of Tempera Painting, 1930–1950. Richard J. Boyle, Hilton Brown and Richard Newman. University of Washington Press. Seattle. 2002.

Painting People. Burt Silverman. Watson-Guptill Publications. New York. 1977.

New Techniques in Egg Tempera. Robert Vickrey. Watson-Guptill Publications. New York. 1989.

The Practice of Tempera Painting. Daniel V. Thompson. Gannon Distributing. Santa Fe, New Mexico. 1986.

SCULPTURE

Sculptors (alphabetically by surname)

Edward Degas: Private Moments: Sculptures. Joseph S. Czestochowski and Anne Pingeot. International Arts. Memphis, Tennessee. 2003.

Auguste Rodin and Camille Claudel. J. Adolf Schmoll Eisenworth. Prestel Publishing. New York. 1999.

The Sculpture of Auguste Rodin: The Collection of the Rodin Museum, Philadelphia. John. L. Tancock. Philadelphia Museum of Art. Philadelphia. 1990.

Rodin: Eros and Creativity. Rainer Crone and Siegfried Salzmann, editors. Prestel Publishing. London. 2006.

Rodin and His Contemporaries: The Iris and B. Gerald Cantor Collection. Albert E. Elsen and Philip Conisbee. Cross River Press. New York. 1992.

Rodin: The Man and His Art. Judith Cladel. The Century Company. New Yrk. 1917.

Rodin: The Shape of Genius. Ruth Butler. Yale University Press. New Haven, Connecticut. 1996.

Per Ung. Per Ung. Labyrinth Press. Oslo, Norway. 1991. (Norwegian)

Sculpting Technique

Modelling and Sculpting the Human Figure. Edouard Lanteri. Dover Publications. New York. 1985.

ARCHITECTURE

Frank Lloyd Wright

Apprentice to Genius: Years with Frank Lloyd Wright. Edgar Tafel. Dover Publications. New York. 1985.

Building with Frank Lloyd Wright: An Illustrated Memoir. Herbert Jacobs and Katherine Jacobs. Southern Illinois University Press. Carbondale, Illinois. 1986.

Details of Frank Lloyd Wright: The California Work, 1909–1974. Judith Dunham, Eric Lloyd Wright and Scot Zimmerman. Chronicle Books. San Francisco. 1994.

Fallingwater: A Frank Lloyd Wright Country House. Edgar Kaufmann, Jr. Abbeville Press. New York. 1986.

Frank Lloyd Wright. Maria Costantino. Random House Value Publishing. New York. 1991.

Frank Lloyd Wright and the Art of Japan: The Architect's Other Passion. Julia Meech. Harry N. Abrams, Inc. New York. 2001.

Frank Lloyd Wright and Colleagues: Indiana Works. Exhibition. July 24–October 24, 1999. John G. Blank Center for the Arts. Michigan City, Indiana. 1999.

The Frank Lloyd Wright Companion, Revised Edition. William A. Storrer. University of Chicago Press. Chicago. 1994.

Frank Lloyd Wright: Design for an American Landscape, 1922–1932. David De Long. Harry N. Abrams, Inc. Italy. 1996.

Frank Lloyd Wright: Hollyhock House and Olive Hill: Buildings and Projects for Aline Barnsdell. Kathryn Smith. Rizzoli International Publications. New York. 1992.

The Future of Architecture. Frank Lloyd Wright. Horizon Press. New York. 1989.

Genius and the Mobocracy. Frank Lloyd Wright. Horizon Press. New York. 1971.

Many Masks: A Life of Frank Lloyd Wright. Brendan Gill. Da Capo Press. Cambridge, Massachusetts. 1998.

My Father Who Is on Earth. John Lloyd Wright *et al.* Southern Illinois University Press. Carbondale, Illinois. 1994.

Other Architects (listed alphabetically by surname)

The Architecture of Arthur Dyson, Second Edition. Mark Hammons. Word Dancer Press. Fresno, California. 1995.

Craig Ellwood: Architecture. Esther McCoy. Hennessey and Ingalls, Inc. Santa Monica, California. 1997.

Irving Gill and the Architecture of Reform: A Study in Modernist Architectural Culture. Thomas S. Hines. Monacelli Press. New York. 2000.

Greene and Greene: Architects in the Residential Style. William R. Current. Morgan and Morgan in cooperation with Amon Carter Museum. Fort Worth, Texas. 1974.

Harwell Hamilton Harris. Lisa Germany. University of California Press. Berkeley, California. 2000.

The Architecture of John Lautner. Alan Hess *et al.* Rizzoli International Publications. New York. 2000.

Lloyd Wright: The Architecture of Frank Lloyd Wright, Jr. Lloyd Wright and Alan Weintraub. Harry N Abrams, Inc. New York. 1998.

Eliel Saarinen: Finnish-American Architect and Educator. Albert Christ-Janer. University of Chicago Press. Chicago. 1985.

Saarinen House and Garden: A Total Work of Art. Gregory Wittkop, editor. Harry N. Abrams, Inc. New York. 1995.

R. M. Schindler. Judith Sheine. Phaidon Press. New York. 2001.

The Autobiography of an Idea. Louis H. Sullivan. Dover Publications. New York. 1956.

The Architectural Theory of Viollet-le-Duc: Readings and Commentary. Eugene-Emmanuel Viollet-le-Duc, edited by M. F. Hearn. MIT Press. Cambridge, Massachussetts. 1990.

Schools and Trends in Architecture

The Adirondack Style. Ann S. O'Leary. Crown Publishing Group. New York. 2002.

Arts and Architecture: The Entenza Years, 1938–1962. Barbara Goldstein, editor. MIT Press. Cambridge, Massachusetts. 1990.

Craftsman Bungalows: 59 Homes from "the Craftsman." Gustav Stickley. Dover Publications. New York, 1989.

The Details of Modern Architecture, Volume 2: 1928–1938. Edward R. Ford. MIT Press. Cambridge, Massachusetts. 1990.

Five California Architects. Esther McCoy. Textbook Publishers. Temecula, California. 2000.

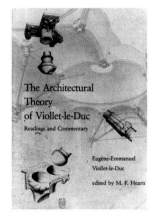

The Geography of Nowhere: The Rise and Decline of America's Man-Made Landscape. James Howard Kunstler. Simon and Schuster. Riverside, New Jersey. 1994.

Louis Sullivan and the Chicago School. Nancy Frazier. Knickerbocker Press. New York. 1999.

Prairie School Architecture: Studies from "The Western Architect." H. Allen Brooks, editor. John Wiley and Sons. Hoboken, New Jersey. 1983.

The Regionalists. Nancy Heller. Watson-Guptill Publications. New York. 1976.

Seaside: Making a Town in America. David Mohney and Keller Easterling. Princeton Architectural Press. New York. 1996.

Seaside Style. Eleanor Lynn Nesmith. Rizzoli International Publications. New York. 2004.

The Use of Land: A Citizen's Policy Guide to Urban Growth. Task Force on Land Use and Urban Growth (Rockefeller Brothers Fund). Crowell Publishing. 1973.

MISCELLANEOUS

The Adirondacks: Views of an American Wilderness. Carl E. Heilman. Rizzoli International Publications. New York. 1999.

The Training of the Memory in Art and the Education of the Artist, Second Edition. Horace Lecoq de Boisbaudran. Macmillan. London. 1914.

Turner's paintings and sculpture were photographed by Craig McClain. Floor plans, site plans and elevations were drawn by Brent Turner. Otherwise, except as noted, illustrations are from the archives of Herbert Turner and the Turner family.

Chapter 3: Art Forms

Paintings

Architecture

Sculpture

Epilogue: Toward a Greener Future

221